Taxation and Red Tape

The Cost to British Business of Complying with
the UK Tax System

D1353947

Taxation and Red Tape

The Cost to British Business of Complying with
the UK Tax System

FRANCIS CHITTENDEN, HILARY FOSTER &
BRIAN SLOAN

The Institute of Economic Affairs

First published in Great Britain in 2010 by
The Institute of Economic Affairs
2 Lord North Street
Westminster
London SW1P 3LB
in association with Profile Books Ltd

The mission of the Institute of Economic Affairs is to improve public understanding of the fundamental institutions of a free society, by analysing and expounding the role of markets in solving economic and social problems.

A CIP catalogue record for this book is available from the British Library.

ISBN 978 0 255 36612 0

Many IEA publications are translated into languages other than English or are reprinted. Permission to translate or to reprint should be sought from the Director General at the address above.

Typeset in Stone by MacGuru Ltd
info@macguru.org.uk

Printed and bound in Great Britain by Hobbs the Printers

CONTENTS

THE AUTHORS

Francis Chittenden

Francis Chittenden is ACCA Professor of Small Business Finance at Manchester Business School. He is a member of the Council of the Association of Chartered Certified Accountants (ACCA). He chairs ACCA's Education Policy and SME Committees and serves on the ACCA Tax Committee. Francis is vice-chair of the SME/SMP working party of the European Federation of Accountants and he is a member of the SME working party of the European Financial Reporting Advisory Group. Professor Chittenden's research interests include the financing of SMEs and the impact of tax and regulation on owner-managed firms. Before becoming an academic, he was a practising accountant, and during this time he founded or co-founded four businesses.

Hilary Foster

Hilary Foster is a Visiting Researcher at Manchester Business School. She has maintained a keen interest in SMEs and owner-managed businesses throughout her career. Her research interests include the key issues for SMEs of growth and cash flow management; and the impact of taxation. Recently she has also undertaken research into environmental taxes and simplification of tax legislation.

Brian Sloan

Dr Brian Sloan is a Visiting Researcher at Manchester Business School. He is a graduate of the School's prestigious doctoral programme and his research interests include government policy towards UK business and the impact of tax and regulation. He has also delivered a series of post-Budget reports and seminars on behalf of the Enterprise Directorate with Francis Chittenden. Brian has consulted for the British Chambers of Commerce on tax, economics and pensions policy, undertaking several successful campaigns on the Chambers' behalf. Prior to undertaking a PhD Brian gained an MBA and achieved Chartered Engineer status after managing and delivering a number of process and product-ivity projects in several manufacturing organisations.

FOREWORD

For years, governments have promised 'bonfires' of regulations and reductions in government bureaucracy, yet it appears that no government initiative in this regard has made significant progress. This study of the UK tax system shows that the burdens of bureaucracy on British businesses can be reduced significantly.

The authors of this monograph carefully distinguish between the costs of government administration on the one hand, and the costs of requirements imposed on the private sector on the other. This distinction is very important. It is quite possible for the government to reduce compliance costs for businesses while building up its own bureaucracy to enforce regulations at greater cost to the general taxpayer. At the same time – and this is a rather more difficult problem to resolve – governments can reduce their own costs while loading more and more costs on to the private sector.

This monograph examines both the costs of administering the tax system and also the costs imposed on firms as informal tax gatherers. The authors review research that has been undertaken throughout the world over twenty years or more. This research is notoriously difficult to conduct and the authors have therefore cross-checked existing research with their own investigations to try to corroborate the various estimates of different aspects of the costs of tax bureaucracy.

The results are alarming. The costs themselves are a huge

burden on business. What is of perhaps greater concern, however, is that the costs weigh sixteen times more heavily on the smallest firms than on the largest. This is a barrier to entrepreneurship, to small-firm formation and to competition.

There have been many incremental attempts to reduce the costs of compliance, but costs simply seem to reappear somewhere else. For example, exemptions from VAT have been widened for small firms and new technologies have been introduced, but, during that period, a whole range of complex tax reliefs have been granted, and also new taxes have been introduced on businesses. Thus, while the costs of collecting taxes have been falling within most OECD countries, in the UK they have remained stagnant.

The authors recommend radical changes both to the structure of the tax system and to its administration. The savings would not be huge compared with total government spending. They would, however, for example, enable the reversal of recent proposed increases in National Insurance Contributions. Furthermore, we should never forget that much is hidden in the averages. While increased efficiencies and reductions in red tape may mean very little for large firms, for firms with no employees the costs of red tape are disproportionately large.

The views expressed in this monograph are, as in all IEA publications, those of the authors and not those of the Institute (which has no corporate view), its managing trustees, Academic Advisory Council Members or senior staff.

PHILIP BOOTH

Editorial and Programme Director,
Institute of Economic Affairs.
Professor of Insurance and Risk Management,
Sir John Cass Business School
January 2010

ACKNOWLEDGEMENTS

This publication has been made possible by the Nigel Vinson Charitable Foundation. The Directors and Trustees of the IEA thank the Rt Hon. Lord Vinson of Roddam Dene LVO for both his intellectual and financial input.

SUMMARY

- The costs of tax collection in the UK are notoriously difficult to estimate but, drawing on recent research, are likely to be of the order of £15–£20 billion.
- The costs imposed on businesses themselves, which have to act as 'informal tax gatherers', are highly regressive. The costs of tax collection bear approximately sixteen times more heavily on the smallest businesses than on the largest. This acts as an impediment to competition and to the expansion of employment among small firms.
- While administrative costs incurred by government are falling in the majority of OECD countries they are not doing so in the UK, despite the introduction of self-assessment and new technologies. Indeed, the UK is one of only three out of the 43 most advanced economies where the costs of tax collection are not falling.
- There is a danger that, as government departments try to be 'more efficient' and are given 'efficiency targets', they impose more costs of tax collection on the private sector.
- Excess government administrative costs and high compliance costs among businesses represent pure economic waste. Realistically, costs could be reduced by between one quarter and one third if there were radical reform of the tax system.
- The UK tax system breaches Adam Smith's canons of

'convenience' and 'efficiency'. These two canons still form an excellent measuring rod for assessing a tax system.

- The average Finance Act in the first decade of this century is over three times as long (463 pages) as the average Finance Act in the 1980s. There is considerable evidence that the volume of legislation affects both the actual and the psychic costs of compliance. Indeed, the UK probably has the longest tax code in the world. At best, it has the second-longest, beaten only by India.

- Although the UK is sixth in the 2009 World Bank 'Ease of doing Business' survey it is ranked sixteenth by ease of paying taxes, having slipped from twelfth in 2008. This is a matter for concern given that 90 per cent of businesses rank the difficulty of paying taxes as one of the top five obstacles to business.

- Radical reform is necessary. For example, taxable and accounting profits should be aligned; special tax reliefs on company investment should be abolished as they impose costs and involve governments in trying to 'pick winners'; and investment returns that are disguised as capital gains should be taxed in the same way that income is taxed, limiting the need to apply Capital Gains Tax at all.

- The annual Finance Act should be abolished. There can then be rigorous analysis of tax laws as and when they need to be passed, rather than a rapid-fire debate which often centres upon 'rabbits' that the Chancellor of the Exchequer has decided to 'pull out of the hat'.

TABLES AND FIGURES

Taxation and Red Tape

The Cost to British Business of Complying with
the UK Tax System

1 INTRODUCTION AND OVERVIEW

This monograph examines the hidden costs to business of taxation and discusses why those costs are important. The focus is the impact on businesses, which include self-employed taxpayers. The starting point for all work in this field is the pioneering research of Cedric Sandford, which remains the most comprehensive study into the area. The hidden costs that we discuss relate to the administrative burden imposed on businesses. It is not the aim of the authors to discuss economic costs caused by a distortion of business activity.

What are the hidden costs of taxation?

Hidden costs in this context are described in the research using the following broad terms:

- Compliance costs – the costs to the taxpayer in complying with the tax system.
- Administration costs – the costs incurred by government in all aspects of revenue collection and administration.

Why do these costs matter?

The compliance and administrative costs of the tax system are

Figure 1   **Government receipts as a percentage of GDP, 1900–2007**

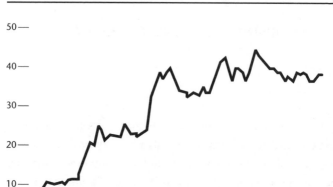

Note: Figures are for general government net receipts on a calendar-year basis.
Sources: T. Clark and A. Dilnot, *Long-term Trends in British Taxation and Spending*, IFS Briefing Note 25, 2002 (www.ifs.org.uk/bns/bn25.pdf); National Statistics series YBHA and ANBY, www. statistics.gov.uk/statbase/tsdtimezone.asp

important because they lead to inefficiency: resources that could be better used to improve economic outcomes are diverted to grapple with the tax system. For example, highly qualified minds are employed to ponder the potato content of snacks (important for applying the correct VAT rate) when they could be producing valuable goods and services.

Boys Smith et al. (2008: 9) highlight the economic problems caused by tax complexity: it makes individuals poorer (because it impairs financial decision-making); it lowers profits and makes markets less efficient (because it increases the deadweight[1]

1   In economic terms, the deadweight loss of taxation is also known as the distortionary cost of taxation. It is the economic loss that society suffers as the result of

cost of taxation and may even discourage new investment from happening at all); it hits small firms hardest (regressivity) because there are economies of scale in tax compliance; and it lowers tax revenues in the long term as a consequence. All of these may also be regarded as hidden costs of taxation – costs to the economy as a whole.

The context of this discussion is that there has been a very significant increase in the extent of total taxation during the twentieth century (in all developed countries). UK total tax revenue as a proportion of GDP since 1900 is shown in Figure 1 above.

Given the impact of the credit crunch on government finances it is likely that taxes will consume an increasing proportion of national income over the next decade. Indeed, government spending is projected to rise to 50 per cent of national income in the next two years, although, in the short run, much of this increase is being financed by borrowing, of course.

Attempts at quantification of costs

One of the difficulties in quantifying the compliance and administrative costs of taxation is the lack of recent comprehensive research. The first detailed estimates were produced by Sandford et al. (1989), relating to 1986/87.

These show an estimated total of £5 billion in 1987 for administrative and compliance costs combined. Note that taxpayer compliance costs were estimated to be more than double the public sector administrative costs at that time.

---

a tax, over and above the revenue it collects. It is assumed that distortions occur because people or firms change their behaviour in order to reduce the amount of tax they must pay.

Table 1 **Tax operating costs, United Kingdom, 1986/87**

	Revenue yield £ billion	Administrative costs %	Compliance costs %	Total costs %
Income tax, CGT, NIC	65	1.5	3.5	5.0
Value Added Tax	21	1.0	3.75	4.75
Corporation Tax	15	0.5	2.25	2.75
Minor taxes	5	0.75	1.5	2.25
Local rates	15	1.5	0.5	2.0
Excise duties	16	0.25	0.25	0.5
Overall average	137	1.25	2.5	3.75
Total costs (£ billion)		1.5	3.5	5.0

Source: Based on Sandford et al. (1989: 192)

It is difficult to show updated figures because:

(i) There have been no updated figures since then and there are no plans to repeat even the 1998 study of the compliance costs of PAYE (known as the Bath Study) that is a subset of the Income Tax, Capital Gains Tax (CGT) and National Insurance Contributions (NIC) above (House of Commons Treasury Committee 2004[2]).

(ii) It would be inappropriate to simply express the figures in today's terms because they are based on the position before the introduction of self-assessment (1996/97), and additionally there have been significant increases in the obligations placed on employers since that time.

---

[2] This report is entitled *The Administrative Costs of Tax Compliance*, and focuses on the extent of the administrative cost of tax compliance placed on business.

According to the House of Commons Treasury Committee report (2004: 6):

> In the absence of firm data it is not possible to determine conclusively how the administrative costs of tax compliance have changed over time. Most business witnesses believed that tax compliance costs, particularly payroll-related costs, have increased. The Revenue Departments considered that compliance costs have been broadly neutral since April 2001. But the Inland Revenue accepted that a number of new payroll requirements had been placed on employers before this, such as the introduction of tax credits, that added significantly to compliance costs. We also note that in reaching its view on compliance costs Customs and Excise specifically excluded measures introduced to combat fraud. We note some evidence which suggested that the administrative costs of tax compliance have risen. But the absence of any reliable method of measurement makes it difficult to adjudicate between these claims. In the absence of any agreed method of measurement these ambiguities will remain.

A key point made in the 2004 report is that the Bath Study (1998) into the costs of PAYE and NIC compliance indicated that these compliance costs were highly regressive, with the highest burden falling on the smallest firms, but the large employers made a 'profit' from their employer responsibilities as a result of the cash-flow holding benefit of paying taxes later than the income that gave rise to the tax liability was received. A number of professional bodies, however, expressed the view to the 2004 review that even those large employers who had previously benefited in this way were likely to now be out of pocket as a result of the increased burden on employers in the last decade. The 2004 report called for a repeat of the Bath Study in order to be able to more accurately measure the changes in these costs over time.

A further important factor since the issue of the report is the 2005 merger of the Inland Revenue and Customs and Excise to form Her Majesty's Revenue and Customs (HMRC). As discussed in a later chapter, this department now faces targets for efficiency savings and there is therefore a temptation to reduce the HMRC administrative costs by transferring these to businesses and thus increasing taxpayer compliance costs.

In 2006 KPMG published their report 'Administrative burdens – HMRC measurement', which was based on 2005 data and measured the administrative burden on business of taxation regulation at £5.1 billion. This figure is analysed further in Chapter 2 and represents, to some extent, an update of the position in the Bath Study across a subset of the categories. Boys Smith et al. (2008) also produced estimates of the amount spent on tax advisers for self-assessment.

For recent estimates of tax administration expenditure incurred by government we can also turn to *Tax Administration in OECD and Selected Non-OECD Countries: Comparative Information Series* (OECD, 2009). The ratio of administrative costs to net revenue collections (costs per 100 units of revenue) is shown for the UK in Table 2. Table 3 shows OECD estimates of the administrative costs of tax collection in total and the percentage of that total that relates to salary costs. These estimates relate only to government costs – not costs imposed on businesses and individuals.

The survey examined data from 30 OECD countries and 13 selected non-OECD countries, 43 countries in total. The UK was in a minority of three countries which had a constant ratio, but

Table 2 **UK ratio of administrative costs to net revenue collections**

2001	2002	2003	2004	2005	2006	2007
1.06	1.11	1.04	0.97	1.10	1.12	1.10

NB: Data to 2004 refer to direct taxes administration. Data from 2005 include
revenue and costs of customs.
Source: OECD (2009: Table 11.1, extract for UK)

for the vast majority of revenue bodies the ratio is decreasing,
perhaps as a result of favourable economic circumstances
(contributing to buoyant tax receipts) and increased efficiency
resulting from technology investments and other initiatives. It is
difficult to carry out international comparisons given the range of
variables to be taken into account, e.g. variations in the range and
nature of taxes collected, differences in the tax rates and overall
tax burden and differences in the underlying cost structures of
revenue bodies. We question, however, why the UK ratio is not
decreasing in line with that of other countries given the efficiency
savings of the merged HMRC and the perceived (by business)
transfer of administrative costs from the public to the private
sector.

Table 3 **Aggregate administrative costs for tax functions, including
salaries and overhead**

UK	2005 £m	2006 £m	2007 £m
Total costs	4,202	4,509	4,773
Salaries	2,648	2,751	2,923
Salaries as % of total	63.0	60.1	61.2

Source: OECD (2009: Table 10, extract for UK)

Summarising the figures above gives an approximation of total operating costs for the UK tax system, shown in Table 4.

Table 4 **Summary of the total operating costs of the UK tax system**

KPMG estimate of business tax administrative burdens	£5.1 billion
OECD estimate of aggregate HMRC administrative costs	£4.8 billion (excluding IT costs, which are outsourced)
Boys Smith et al. estimate of amount spent on tax advisers by those subject to self-assessment	£1.25 billion
The total of these gives us a starting point for total combined administrative and compliance costs (operating costs)	£11 billion+

We believe that if comprehensive research were to be carried out (e.g. an update of the Sandford research) the total would be found to be much higher, as is discussed further in Chapter 4. Table 4 does not cover all the categories of taxation analysed in the Sandford research. For comparison purposes the total HMRC receipts for 2008/09 are reported as £438.617 billion. If we apply the percentage calculated by Sandford in 1986/87 for total administrative and compliance costs of 3.75 per cent, this would give a projected total of £16.5 billion costs, but given the increased complexity of the UK tax system since then we believe the final total is likely to be higher still.

Overview of remaining chapters

After this brief introduction to the problem, Chapter 2 examines the concept of the hidden costs of taxation and reviews definitions from the literature. Compliance costs incurred by the private sector are more difficult to define and there is disagreement among scholars as to whether certain elements (for example, psychological costs) should be included. Administrative costs (public sector costs) are generally more straightforward to estimate because the majority of costs are staff-related. The combined compliance and administrative costs are referred to as 'Operating costs of the tax system'. In this context the term 'Burden' is given the same sense as in the Administrative Burdens Measurement Exercise, i.e. it refers to the burden on business in complying with the tax requirements.

After noting the difficulties of definition, the challenges of measurement are then explored. With all aspects, much of the compliance cost is attributable to time or labour costs. It is clear that underlying all the discussion is the fact that many of the costs are due to a combination of factors: change, complexity, and how HMRC responds at an operational level to its customers.

Chapter 3 traces the history and context of research into the hidden costs of taxation. Despite the identification by Adam Smith of a cost obligation other than the incidence of a tax itself, research into compliance costs (the hidden costs of taxation) had been neglected by governments and academics alike until the mid-to-late twentieth century. With few notable exceptions it was not until the work of Sandford (1973) that research in this field gained momentum.

Chapter 4 describes the changing environment that has to a large extent forced the hand of government in tackling the issue of costs of compliance with all legislative and regulatory requirements, of which the costs of complying with the tax regime form a significant part.

Chapter 5 examines progress in reducing administrative

burdens. There has been recognition by governments worldwide of the need to reduce the administrative burdens caused by legislation, of which the costs of complying with the tax system are a part. This has become and seems set to remain an important part of the political agenda: 'The level of attention being given by member countries to administrative burden reduction is currently on a scale not previously witnessed' (OECD, 2008: 45).

Chapter 6 provides a composite view of the current state of the UK tax system informed by academic writing in the field, focus groups we have held in the course of related research, and the authors' own experience in industry and as advisers to small businesses. We believe that the UK tax system is currently in turmoil and there is a lack of trust on both sides, and this has increased following the revelations regarding MPs' expenses and alleged tax avoidance activities in the spring of 2009. Practitioners and small businesses regard politicians and the Treasury as being out of touch with how businesses operate; equally, government and the tax authorities are suspicious of businesses, believing they will go to great lengths to avoid paying tax (Williams, 2008).

In the final chapter we examine the issue of complexity in the UK tax system, noting the trend in possibly simplistic measures, such as the number of pages of primary legislation and the increases in the number of pages in each successive year's Finance Act. We examine the likely reasons for the increase in complexity and trace the history of calls for simplification and finally suggest ways in which complexity could be reduced.

During our discussions, we have seen that the chief contributory factor to the increasing hidden costs of taxation is complexity, both in the tax legislation and in the workings of the tax system. Additionally, we believe that in order to substantially reduce compliance costs and the distortions they create, a fundamental rethink of the tax system is needed. The task of reducing administrative and compliance costs therefore requires a multi-faceted approach. There appears to be general agreement about the drivers of complexity and unpredictability in tax systems (as discussed by Boys Smith et al. (2008: 17)), and these apply equally to direct and indirect taxes. The drivers of complexity appear to be:

- The weight of past legislation.
- The desire to prevent tax avoidance.
- The temptation to use tax to micro-manage society.
- The pressure on the Chancellor to 'do something' on an annual basis.
- The desire to raise taxes in a way that will be less obvious to the taxpayer (and thus minimise the outcry by lobbying factions).
- The problem of lack of scrutiny before tax policy is enacted, leading to mistakes and lack of stability and trust in the tax system (if not the political process as a whole).

To address these problems we propose a major simplification of existing legislation and a number of further reforms.

2 WHAT ARE THE HIDDEN COSTS OF TAXATION AND WHY DO THEY MATTER?

Introduction

As long as there have been taxes there have been costs associated with remitting and collecting them beyond the tax liability itself. Adam Smith identified a number of ways in which tax systems fail to meet the principle behind his fourth canon of taxation (see below) and concluded that 'taxes are frequently so much more burdensome to the people than they are beneficial to the sovereign' (Smith, 1776).

Early in the twentieth century, when there were fewer taxpayers (perhaps about 5 per cent of the population), the total costs of collecting taxes were relatively small. As taxes rose, however, the numbers of individuals required to pay taxes increased, resulting in greater costs of administration and compliance. Additionally, as modern tax systems have developed they have imposed an increasing burden on taxpayers and particularly on business taxpayers (Evans, 2001). It is probably no coincidence that interest in ascertaining the nature and quantity of these costs became more urgent in the latter half of the twentieth century, as demonstrated by Sandford's pioneering work in this area.

Although these costs are described as 'hidden' costs, the regular outcry from business when legislation changes suggests that it is not their existence as such which is hidden, but rather their extent and quantification which are not immediately obvious.

Hidden costs arise under two main headings: first, costs to the taxpayer in complying with the tax system (private sector compliance costs) and, second, costs incurred by government in all aspects of revenue collection and administration (public sector administration costs). Note that estimates of these costs should be based not only on normal transactions but also on when things go wrong (Bennett et al., 2009: 5).

Another descriptive term is 'operating costs' (Sandford et al., 1989: 22; Evans, 2001: 5), which is intended to describe the combined administrative and compliance costs of operating the tax system for both taxpayers and government. In practice a number of terms are used to describe these costs and their nature, such as 'direct and indirect costs'; 'internal and external costs'; 'fixed and variable costs'; and 'recurring and non-recurring costs'. There is still no universal agreement on a definition of compliance costs or even which elements should be included in the calculation of compliance costs (Chittenden et al., 2002: 2).

A UK definition of tax compliance costs is: 'the costs which are incurred by taxpayers or third parties in meeting the require-ments of the tax system, over and above the tax liability itself and over and above any harmful distortions of consumption or production to which the tax may give rise' (Sandford et al., 1981: 13). The focus, then, is clear: this monograph centres on taxpayers' compliance costs and not the tax liability itself, nor the economic distortions arising as a result of the operation of any specific tax.

Tax administrative costs are defined as the 'costs incurred by the revenue authorities in the taxation process' (ibid.: 13). This may encompass a wide range of public sector costs, including staffing the various departments required to administer the tax system, collection of taxes and the appeals system, and the element of interest-free loans arising as a result of cash-flow benefits to businesses that are able to delay tax payments in VAT or PAYE systems.

This chapter explores the nature of these hidden costs, including attempts at quantification, and their importance to society and the economy. Therefore the focus is on business taxes both as applied to individuals (the self-employed and unincorporated businesses which pay Income Tax) and to companies (incorporated businesses that pay Corporation Tax).

In this context 'business' is taken to mean all forms of business from the self-employed, moving through larger unincorporated but employing businesses through to the separate legal entity of an incorporated business or limited company.

Outline of the hidden costs of compliance
Private sector compliance costs

Businesses face numerous taxes, not just Corporation Tax (for incorporated business) or Income Tax (for the self-employed and partnerships), but also PAYE and NIC (for employing businesses); VAT; Business Rates; excise duties; stamp duties; and specific product taxes such as insurance tax, airport taxes and fuel duties (i.e. environmental taxes). For the taxpayer there are compliance costs associated with each of these, and those costs may vary with the characteristics of the specific tax and also according to the size of the business.

In general terms, compliance costs may be described as those costs a taxpayer incurs in attempting to comply with a given tax.

Although there is much disagreement about what should be included, there are certain costs which are clearly part of the tax compliance process. Evans (2001: 5) lists these as follows:

- The costs of labour/time consumed in completion of tax activities. For example, the time taken by a business person to acquire appropriate knowledge to deal with tax obligations such as PAYE or VAT; or the time taken in compiling receipts and recording data in order to be able to complete a tax return.
- The costs of expertise purchased to assist with completion of tax activities (typically, the fees paid to professional tax advisers).
- Incidental expenses incurred in completion of tax activities, including computer software, postage, travel, etc.

The literature has also identified 'psychic' (or psychological) costs of compliance. Sandford et al. (1989: 18) found that psychic costs are experienced by many taxpayers. Although difficult to measure, he found that 'many people experience considerable anxiety or frustration in dealing with their tax affairs; some employ a professional advisor primarily to reduce this burden of worry. In so far as this has the desired effect, the psychic cost then becomes a monetary cost'.

For the business community in particular, as complexity in the tax system increases it seems reasonable to suppose that there is a consequent rise in the level of the burden of worry. Furthermore, Sandford et al. (ibid.: 18) also noted that there may also be 'psychic administrative costs' for tax officials if they find their dealings with the public stressful.

There may also be 'social costs', which some writers regard as bordering with efficiency costs – for example, where a tax change, such as the introduction of a higher rate of VAT on a particular range of goods, causes a trader to cease to stock those goods (in order to keep tax affairs simple), thereby inconveniencing customers who have to travel farther to continue to buy those goods (ibid.: 19; Evans, 2001: 5).

Furthermore, a confrontational stance by the tax authorities may increase compliance costs among all taxpayers (honest as well as evaders) because honest taxpayers, fearing an investigation, will 'spend undue time to ensure their records are meticulous' (Sandford et al., 1989: 203).

Sandford et al. (ibid.: 12) also discuss the distinction made (by Johnston, 1961) in the literature between 'unavoidable (or mandatory) costs', e.g. those costs necessary for the taxpayer to meet the legal requirements imposed by the tax; and 'avoidable (or voluntary) costs', e.g. tax planning, which the taxpayer chooses to incur in order to minimise the liability. The point is also made, however, that neither of these costs would exist in the absence of the tax, and therefore Sandford argues that these discretionary costs could legitimately be included as costs of compliance. In the end he proposes the concept of 'the costs which a reasonable man would incur', thereby recognising that many taxpayers merely seek to avoid 'tax traps in a genuine commercial transaction', and suggesting that the costs of artificial tax minimisation schemes in total are likely to be very small in relation to compliance costs as a whole.

In the case where an owner-manager is responsible for their own tax affairs, a further opportunity cost may arise: that of the loss to the economy of that individual's time in dealing with tax issues as opposed to developing the business. We suggest there are both financial and psychic costs for self-employed and unincorporated businesses: financial in the sense that if the proprietor deals with their own tax affairs, the cost of their time is not deductible for tax purposes; psychic in the sense that, given the many demands on them (including regulatory demands, as we discuss in a later chapter), they have a limited time to find the relevant information, and take the required actions with regard to tax matters, and therefore may retain a nagging uncertainty as to whether they have fulfilled their obligations and made optimal decisions.

Costs moving from public to private sector

Modern tax systems are very different in structure and purpose from the system in place at the start of the twentieth century, when the tax take was typically around 10 per cent of national income. As the tax take rose, the introduction of PAYE proved advantageous to government both in terms of improved cash flow during the tax year and because employers acted as collection agents. This system was quite efficient when most people worked for large public or private sector organisations (Lymer and Oats, 2008: 16). Additionally, the electorate became used to the idea of paying tax as a deduction from salary. Indeed, for 2006/07 the UK government's largest source of tax revenue was that collected through the PAYE system: £125 billion in Income Tax and £85 billion in National Insurance Contributions (NAO, 2007).

It is clear that the responsibility for operating this part of the tax system falls to employers and they bear the lion's share of the cost. Further analysis reveals, however, that there may also be benefits in terms of a cash-flow advantage to employers arising out of operating this system, because the employer deducts tax and National Insurance from employees on one date and pays it over to HMRC at a later date.

It could be argued that the government has passed these costs across to the private sector, so that although in one sense the public sector costs may be viewed as having decreased, the total combined cost may not have reduced. The cash-flow benefit for businesses is a cost for government, however, as it is effectively an interest-free loan to businesses. So that overall the cost may balance the benefit for some businesses – particularly larger businesses.

Whiting (2003) explains that when PAYE was introduced in 1944 it was a simple system, did not apply to everyone and had the cash-flow benefit as a trade-off. He notes that since that time there have been significant changes both in employment patterns and the complexity of the tax system: 'When you start trying to make the system cope with things that it was not designed for, too much of a burden is placed on employers who are expected to work out all the tax implications for the Revenue – and who get penalised if they get it wrong.'

He sounds a warning against increasing the burden on employers, reasoning that they may react by creating fewer jobs, leading to increased self-employment, which will, in turn, increase the pressure on the system: a prediction that has come to pass!

In the UK the operation of the VAT system may also give a cash-flow benefit to businesses; for those firms at the smaller end of the scale, however, there are issues to be faced when they first cross the registration threshold (see below).

Public sector administration costs

The government incurs hidden costs in the administration and collection of taxes. As with the definition of what should be included when measuring compliance costs, a similar debate continues with how administrative costs should be measured. An obvious example of these is the cost of running and maintaining revenue offices, including accommodation, salary and pensions costs relating to the staff of Revenue departments. In addition, an attempt to measure the total public sector costs of the tax system should also include the costs of introducing a tax or making major modifications to it (Sandford et al., 1989: 3).

Evans (2001: 5) cites the less obvious administrative costs: the costs of legislative enactment relating to the tax system, from initial policy formulation through to statutory or other rule enactment; also the judicial costs of administration of the tax dispute system, which may involve local and national tribunals and – in the extreme – the courts.

Other potential costs for inclusion are interest-free loans to the private sector, either because of specified collection periods (e.g. under the VAT and PAYE systems) or because of late payment of liabilities by taxpayers.

After considering these items, Sandford et al. (1989: 5), recognising the difficulties of drawing a precise border, define the structure of public sector costs as those costs 'incurred in administering an existing tax code (including advice on its modification)'. They choose to exclude the majority of costs related to new legislation and interpretation of the law, and legal interest-free loans (this latter, they suggest, would be very small).

Evans (2001: 5) believes, however, that although the above definition allows for simplicity of measurement, there are strong grounds for including legislative and judicial costs in calculations of administrative costs where they are available and where they clearly relate to the governmental costs of administering the tax system.

Legal interest-free loans are discussed in more detail below. The costs attributable to interest-free loans due to late payment by taxpayers are disregarded as it is considered they would be cancelled out by interest and penalties charged (Sandford et al., 1989).

Gross and net compliance costs

It is worth noting the distinction between gross and net compliance costs. The notion of net compliance costs refers to the offset from spin-off benefits, e.g. better systems implemented as a result of the need to comply which give the added benefit to businesses of improved management information and the cash-flow benefits as a result of operating PAYE and VAT systems.

Measurement of hidden costs

Having enumerated the difficulties in defining the component parts of administrative and compliance costs, the next challenge is to obtain a measurement of those costs. The difficulty of measuring this burden until comparatively recently has been the lack of availability of data, particularly with regard to taxpayer compliance costs.

Measurement of compliance costs

Sandford et al. (ibid.: 10) identify the direct and quantifiable costs incurred by taxpayers in meeting the requirements of tax legislation as follows:

> … for individuals, the cost of acquiring sufficient knowledge to meet their legal requirements; of compiling the necessary receipts and other data and of completing tax returns; payments to professional advisers for tax advice; and incidental costs of postage, telephone and travel in order to communicate with tax advisers or the tax office. For a business, the compliance costs include the costs of collecting, remitting and accounting for tax on the products or profits of the business and on the wages and salaries of its employees together with the costs of acquiring the knowledge to enable this work to be done including knowledge of their legal obligations and penalties …

In valuing compliance costs, Sandford et al. (ibid.: 35) highlight labour cost as a major component of compliance cost, i.e. the time taken by people in order to carry out compliance activities. Four main categories are identified: the time of professional advisers; the time of employees doing tax compliance work for an employer; the time of business owners and the self-employed doing tax compliance work in connection with their own business; and the time of individuals doing their own personal tax work in what would otherwise be leisure time.

The first two are relatively straightforward: the time of professional advisers is represented by the fee charged (the cost to the client and the resource cost to the economy), the only complication being where a fee includes services other than tax, which may not always be easy to analyse; valuation of an employee's time is generally agreed to be represented by the time taken at the employee's wage rate together with employment costs, e.g. National Insurance and pension contributions. This represents both the cost to the employer and the resource cost to the economy. The time of the self-employed is more difficult to value as it is not straightforward to obtain an opportunity cost for the individual's time. Possible measures are the individual's average rate of remuneration and the charge-out rate.

It is more difficult to value lost leisure time of individuals because this will vary according to individuals' attitudes. It is also worth noting that it will often be the spouse of the small business proprietor who will undertake tax compliance work (e.g. VAT returns).

It is also important to bear in mind the regressivity of compliance costs. The total for compliance costs does not tell the full story given their distribution over different sizes of firms. As discussed below, studies have found that small firms bear a proportionately higher burden of compliance costs than larger firms.

Measurement of psychic or psychological costs

Sandford recognised that psychic costs 'whilst difficult or impossible to measure satisfactorily are an important component of compliance costs' (ibid.: 18). Where the taxpayer pays a professional to undertake this work and thus removes the psychic burden, then to this extent the psychic cost becomes quantifiable. Woellner et al. (2001: 37) suggest that a significant contributory factor to psychic costs is the complexity of the tax legislation.

As Western countries have ever increasing demands for more revenue and taxpayers try to minimise the amount of tax they pay, a vicious cycle develops. Taxpayers find a loophole, which is upheld by the courts, complicated (and at times almost unworkable) legislation is introduced to close the loophole, and the compliance costs of all stakeholders in the tax system increase as a result of the commensurate increase in legislative complexity.

They suggest that there is an overlap between time costs and psychological costs, because the less user-friendly the legislation, the longer it takes to interpret and apply and consequently the more it costs to comply.

This Australian team (ibid.) undertook a qualitative study to attempt to measure psychic costs, which they define as 'the mental and emotional costs, anxiety and stress which taxpayers or advisors experience when dealing with the tax legislation'. The motivation for the study was to evaluate whether the attempts since 1993 by the Australian government to simplify the tax legislation had reduced compliance costs. Three tests were used: a series of carefully selected focus groups in which issues relating to compliance costs were discussed; persons in different categories solved practical case studies using legislation written under the old and the 'new' drafting style; and the use of a 'read aloud' protocol in which participants documented verbally each step in their attempts to solve the practical case study allotted to them. A pilot study of university students was also conducted, half of whom had studied tax for two semesters, the remainder having never studied tax.

The study was qualitative in nature and noted the psychological reactions of participants. A disturbing finding was that no one solved the set problem, and the trial confirmed that 'tax legislation is impossible even for tertiary trained tax students to deal with without resorting to secondary sources'.

Psychic costs may also be influenced by the attitude of the revenue authority. If a confrontational attitude is adopted by the revenue authority this is likely to increase the stress levels and thus the psychic costs of the taxpayer.

Measurement of administrative costs

Sandford et al. (1989: 6) enumerate the contents of administrative (HMRC) costs: '… salaries and wages of staff at all levels, including national insurance contributions and superannuation costs; accommodation costs (including rents, rates, heating, lighting and cleaning); postage, telephone, printing, stationery; travel, computing and other equipment costs'.

In the UK, there is a requirement for HMRC to publish data on the administrative costs of central government taxes. The Financial Management Initiative (FMI), formally introduced in 1982, has resulted in the availability of a detailed breakdown of costs analysed between specific aspects of the service (e.g. investigative activities) and with regard to individual taxes and groups of taxes.

Sandford et al. (ibid.: 7) note difficulties with the data, e.g. insufficient analysis of the costs of administering duties on alcoholic drinks. They also describe general problems with regard to the nature of government costings in terms of the amounts and their allocation over time, and discuss the difficulty of obtaining appropriate opportunity costs. Ultimately they conclude that these problems are likely to be insignificant given the high proportion (70 per cent) of staff-related costs.

According to recent data, the administrative costs of HMRC have substantially reduced in terms of 'costs of collection', from about £1.70 per £100 in 1995/96 to £1.10 per £100 collected in 2005/06, although this is due in part to the inclusion of new revenue lines (NICs and VAT) in the 'costs of collection' computation, as revenue collection operations have been further integrated (Highfield, 2008)[1] and efficiency savings implemented.

Why are hidden costs important?

To ensure that taxes can be enforced and collected governments must introduce legislation and bestow powers upon their respective revenue collection authorities. Inevitably legislation and powers lead to regulation and audit requirements on taxpayers that increase the hidden costs associated with taxation. Adam Smith claimed that over-regulation and expensive administration restricted economic development, and two of his four Canons of Taxation can be interpreted as establishing a principle of minimising the operating costs of the tax system (Smith, 1776). The two canons are:

Convenience – 'Every tax ought to be levied at a time, or in the manner, most convenient for the contributor to pay it.'

Efficiency – 'Every tax ought to be so contrived as both to take out, and keep out, of the pockets of the people, as little as possible over and above what it brings in to the public treasury of the state. A tax may either take out or keep out of the pockets of the people a

---

1   Later figures indicate that the UK ratio remains more or less constant at this level: £1.12 per £100 collected in 2006/07 and £1.10 per £100 collected in 2007/08 (OECD, 2009). As noted in Chapter 1, however, many other countries have decreased their ratio.

great deal more than it brings into the public treasury, and in four ways: a) by the number of officers who levy it; b) by obstructing the industry of the people; c) by penalties incurred in attempting to evade tax; d) by subjecting the people to the frequent visits and examinations of the tax-gatherers.'

Thus 'convenience' suggests that it should be easy for taxpayers to comply with the system, and 'efficiency' is concerned with minimising government's costs of administering the tax. Of course, any administrative costs incurred by government are ultimately borne by all taxpayers as additional tax must be raised to cover them. These two canons also present the first insight into a difficult issue concerning the debate over the hidden costs of taxation and what is being measured.

The discussion above explores the difficulty of defining and measuring tax compliance costs. A subset of compliance costs are Administrative Burdens, which estimate the time costs of a 'normally efficient business' in collecting and providing to government information required by regulation. Administrative burdens are an issue that has been of increasing concern to governments, and the aim of reducing administrative burdens is an item on the political agenda of many OECD member countries. 'Nowhere is the challenge greater than in the area of taxation which is consistently identified by business as the key area of concern from an administrative burden viewpoint' (OECD, 2008: 5).

In the UK, an Administrative Burdens Measurement Exercise (ABME) has been carried out by KPMG LLP (2006) working with HMRC, and although the UK was reportedly found to compare favourably with other European countries, realistically the ABME estimates lack the rigour necessary to allow comparison between countries, or even within a single country across time. There remain issues for business in terms of tax forms and returns as well as audit and inspections.

Nevertheless, the KPMG study (ibid.: 4) does give an overview of the UK tax administrative burden on business. They concluded:

> The administrative burden of UK tax regulation is £5.1 billion. Of this, 41% represents internal costs (that is, the costs of activities that business undertakes in order to be compliant), 49% represents external costs (the costs of working with intermediaries) and 9% represents acquisition costs (the non-time costs incurred by business). The split among these three types of costs varies considerably among tax areas. The key factors that influence the level of use of intermediaries seem to be the complexity of the tax regulation (that is, the need to understand the regulation), the number of businesses affected (that is, the size of the potential market for intermediaries) and the extent to which the regulation goes to the heart of a business's operations (that is, the need to understand the business operations). As a general principle, the greater the complexity of tax regulation and the greater the number of businesses affected, the greater the use of intermediaries.

Table 5 on page 46 summarises the KPMG findings.

Within the study KPMG described three aspects of burden: the burden created by change; the burden created by complexity; and the burden created by 'grit in the system': that is, how HMRC responds at an operational level to its customers. These echo the contributory factors to psychic costs described by Woellner et al. above.

Adam Smith makes the case that inefficiency in collecting taxes has detrimental effects in general, but a disaggregation of the data gives us greater insights.

Table 5 **Administrative burden by business size**

	Total administrative burden on businesses					
	Nano	Micro	Small	Medium	Large	Total
	0	1–9	10–49	50–249	250+	
	employees	employees	employees	employees	employees	
Number of businesses	2,996,983	957,370	166,499	33,300	8,325	4,162,477
Tax area	£m	£m	£m	£m	£m	£m
VAT	160	344	166	94	256	1,020
Income tax for businesses	511	230	60	51	5	857
Customs	242	126	366	48	12	793
Employer taxes	0	523	131	47	59	759
Corporation Tax	2	267	89	76	175	608
Construction Industry Scheme	96	181	37	6	1	321
Pensions	–	186	41	14	53	294
Capital allowances	90	42	12	5	2	151
Environmental taxes	0	0	3	4	20	26
Other	115	53	20	19	60	267
Total taxes	1,216	1,952	925	364	643	5,100
% burden by business size	23.84	38.27	18.14	7.14	12.61	100.00

Source: Based on the KPMG ABME report (KPMG LLP 2006: 27) using 2005 data from the Small Business Service (SBS) and HMRC. (NB: the table does not cross-total owing to rounding errors in the original publication.)

Regressivity

A review of the evidence on the regulatory burden in the USA, the UK, the EU, Australia and New Zealand (Chittenden et al., 2002: 49) found broad agreement about a number of key facts related to the measurement of the burden of compliance. In general terms all countries recognised that small firms bear a relatively higher burden of costs than larger businesses. It was harder to judge the extent to which the burden was disproportionate, however, because the way in which data in the studies had been produced did not lend itself to this kind of interpretation. In those cases where data was produced by business-size band, there was variation in categorisation and measures of size and also in the nature of the small business sector itself.

Where the differential impact could be quantified, they concluded that the general regulatory burden faced by businesses with up to twenty employees was at least 35 per cent higher than that for the largest size of firm. In the specific area of taxation, large firms were seen to benefit because of the interaction of economies of scale and cash-flow benefits. As a result small firms may bear compliance costs that are several times larger than the costs borne by large firms, thus indicating the regressive nature of these costs.

Indeed, a number of studies have reported the disproportionate tax burden on smaller firms (European Commission, 2007; Chittenden et al., 2002). Two factors are cited as responsible for this: first, compliance costs are largely fixed, and second, larger companies are more efficient at dealing with tax compliance because the larger sums involved allow for the use of specialists and investment in software to increase efficiency (European Commission, 2007: 5). According to the Commission: 'European SMEs have a cost to tax revenue ratio (i.e. the ratio between total tax-related compliance costs and paid taxes) of 30.9%. Large companies on the other hand have a cost to tax revenue ratio of only 1.9%' (ibid.: 12). The effect can be multiplied where the state seeks to apply special rules to smaller firms.

In the UK in particular, there are a number of complexities in the tax legislation which arise out of a wish by government to encourage particular activities. This complexity contributes to costs on all levels: objective costs of compliance; time taken to compile information and complete returns; payment for tax advice; and psychic costs resulting from the frustration of dealing with ever-increasing complexity. To illustrate this point, commenting specifically on the problems with IR35, Freedman (2008) states: '... the legislation is hard to enforce, probably raises little revenue, and yet creates compliance costs and concerns for far more taxpayers than are actually caught by the rules'.

The KPMG ABME data report (KPMG LLP, 2006) did not make it entirely clear how regressive tax administration costs are. Yet the novel analysis that follows demonstrates that even the information obligations faced by normally efficient firms are particularly regressive.

By using the number of firms in the economy estimated in the KPMG study and the administration burden totals by size of firm, based on number of employees, an average administration burden can be established, as shown in Table 6.

The Department for Business Innovation and Skills[2] does provide a total turnover for all firms by size. The typical turnover of a firm by number of employees can be established for the start of 2006 (closest to the KPMG study period). The outcome of this is shown below in Table 7.

---

2   Private sector firms based on the Enterprise Directorate's statistics for the start of 2006. Available at http://stats.berr.gov.uk/ed/sme/index.htm, last accessed 17 November 2009.

Table 6 **Administrative burdens by size of firm**

	Nano	Micro	Small	Medium	Large	Weighted average
Employees	Zero	1–9	10–49	50–249	250+	All firms
Number of businesses	2,996,983	957,370	166,499	33,300	8,325	4,162,477
Total administrative burdens (millions)	1,216	1,952	925	364	643	5,100
Average admin. burden, £	406	2,039	5,556	10,931	77,237	1,225

Source: KPMG LLP (2006)

Table 7 **Typical turnover by size of firm for start of 2006**

	Nano	Micro	Small	Medium	Large	Weighted average
Employees	Zero	1–9	10–49	50–249	250+	All firms
Number of businesses	3,262,715	1,005,535	165,980	26,530	5,940	4,466,700
Total turnover (millions)	207,615	384,504	379,891	385,751	1,256,146	2,613,907
Average turnover, £	63,633	382,387	2,288,776	14,540,181	211,472,391	585,199

Source: Enterprise Directorate statistics for start of 2006

When the figures in Tables 6 and 7 are combined the following results in Table 8 are obtained, showing that the average administration burden of taxes is 0.21 per cent of turnover: this is higher for firms employing fewer than 50 people. The smallest firms have a burden of 0.64 per cent of turnover, but the burden is only 0.04 per cent for the largest firms. This clearly demonstrates the regressive nature of tax compliance on businesses, even for those normally efficient businesses that were selected for the UK government's own study. A figure of 0.64 per cent of turnover may seem like a small sum. With a profit margin of, for example, 10 per cent, however, this implies that the cost of *complying* with taxes is nearly 7 per cent of total profits – it is a much higher proportion of post-tax profits, of course.

Table 8 **Administration burdens as a percentage of turnover**

	Nano	Micro	Small	Medium	Large	Weighted average
Employees	Zero	1–9	10–49	50–249	250+	All firms
Administration burden as % turnover	0.64	0.53	0.24	0.08	0.04	0.21

Links between compliance costs and voluntary compliance

There is a suggestion (Hasseldine, 2001) that compliance costs may have an effect on voluntary compliance, although specific research has yet to be undertaken. The reasoning is that if a government communicates its attempts to reduce complexity and compliance costs, then levels of compliance may increase. Hasseldine theorises that a significant part of the problem of tax non-compliance may be attributable to the complexities of tax laws and high compliance costs, and he recommends that researchers should explore the linkages between tax compliance research and tax compliance costs research.

A related consequence is that the compliance costs of taxation may affect business decisions. For example, with regard to the VAT system there are two reasons why businesses not registered for VAT deliberately delay growth (Chittenden et al., 2005: 639). First, they may do so in order not to exceed the VAT registration limit and thus avoid the compliance costs associated with the VAT system. Second, when a trader is coming up to the VAT threshold, they have to increase their turnover significantly to actually stand still, because, if they cross over the VAT threshold, they then suddenly lose in tax 17.5 per cent of the value-added in the business. So there is seen to be a real problem, particularly around the VAT threshold.

As regards the PAYE system, there is evidence (ibid.: 639) that the cost of operating the system deters some small firms from taking on their first employee.

We suggest that both of these strategies may have a detrimental effect on enterprise at the individual business level and for the economy as a whole.

Spin-off benefits

There are suggestions that tax compliance may result in benefits for business. Evans (2001: 6) notes that tax compliance activities may result in managerial benefits such as better accounts and record-keeping and may lead to improved business decision-making. Crawford and Freedman (2008: 47) suggest that 'the tax requirement bolsters a commercial need, for example, to keep proper accounts'. This is not to say that businesses would necessarily choose to meet the cost of keeping such complex records but, given that they have to, they have a positive value.

This may not always be the case, however, as KPMG LLP (2006: 5) report:

> The biggest single activity business has to carry out is
> information gathering: finding the information needed to
> be compliant. This information is often not readily available
> from accounting systems. This being the case, businesses

incur costs in finding the underlying data behind the accounting system or by investing in reconfiguring their accounting systems.

This suggests that the tax compliance cost may be additional to normal management activities, and a further statement in support of this view was made by the Institute of Directors: 'to some extent, any business is going to have to record some information for financial reporting, for other purposes, but a large part of the reporting requirements for tax goes way above and beyond what most businesses would require' (House of Commons Treasury Committee, 2004: 7).

As discussed above, there may also be cash-flow benefits to employers from operating a PAYE system for employees. Indeed, Sandford et al. (1989: 90) found that overall the compliance costs of collecting PAYE and NIC were wiped out by the cash-flow benefit owing to the timing of payments. Closer examination revealed, however, the regressive nature of these compliance costs, as the largest firms had net negative compliance costs (the cash-flow benefit exceeded the compliance costs) but the small and medium-sized firms had positive net costs which were proportionately heavier for the small firm. Furthermore, comments made in the House of Commons Treasury Committee report (2004: 12) suggest that the large firms may now also be out of pocket as a result of the considerable increase in the employer burden since the Bath Study was carried out.

Conclusion

Compliance costs are generally agreed to be the costs incurred by taxpayers in complying with the tax system, although there is disagreement among scholars as to whether certain elements such as psychological costs should be included. Administrative costs, incurred by the government, are generally more straightforward to estimate because the majority of costs are staff-related. The combined compliance and administrative costs are referred to as 'operating costs of the tax system'. There are difficulties in measuring both main aspects of operating costs. It is clear that many of the costs are due to a combination of factors: change, complexity, and how HMRC responds at an operational level to its customers. It appears likely that all operating costs of the tax system are influenced by these factors.

It is clear that compliance costs (private sector costs) are regressive in nature, with a disproportionate burden being borne by small firms. There is also evidence that the compliance costs of taxation may affect the business decisions of small firms to the extent that they increase operating costs, divert resources away from value-adding activities and delay growth and employment. These issues are of particular significance for an economy that is concerned to promote enterprise and encourage small firms.

3 HISTORY AND CONTEXT OF RESEARCH INTO THE HIDDEN COSTS OF TAXATION

Introduction

In what is now seen as the seminal work looking into the hidden costs of taxation, the burden of taxation is often classified into four categories (Sandford, 1973):

- Tax payments, in particular excessive taxation that can lead to inefficient allocation of resources.
- Costs from price distortion.
- Administrative costs incurred by the public sector in collecting taxes and administering the tax system.
- Compliance costs incurred by taxpayers in meeting their obligation to pay tax.

Before Sandford's work there are few notable contributions to be found in the literature. There is now, however, a considerable body of research concerning the compliance costs of taxation in many developed nations, including the UK, the USA, Australia and New Zealand.

This monograph concerns the hidden costs of taxation that are borne by business taxpayers: therefore it is compliance costs which are of interest. As noted in the previous chapter, however, the definitions of compliance costs and administrative costs have become somewhat blurred, particularly by the administrative burdens terminology increasingly being used by governments.[1]

In this chapter the hidden costs of taxation are considered from a historical perspective to inform the reader of the background to current developments, future trends and the policy implications. The scale of the impact of the hidden costs of taxation has become increasingly important as the number of taxpayers has increased. In the UK, for example, Income Tax in the early twentieth century was paid by fewer than a million of the more wealthy individuals (Lymer and Oats, 2008); by the end of the century, however, the majority of the working population faced some form of Income Tax liability. The number and types of taxes have also increased over this period, with the introduction of Corporation Tax and taxes such as National Insurance Contributions that were hypothecated at the time of introduction. These trends are also evident in many other countries. The structure of the tax system itself has also been transformed, with the introduction of many forms of indirect taxation, levied on consumption and expenditure.

Methods for measuring the scale and impact of taxation have developed over time, with many advances made by Sandford (1973). Chittenden et al. (2003) describe elements of the costs measured in compliance cost studies. They point out that disagreements arise over the methodological issues related to the studies and that the ways researchers ask their questions can influence the compliance cost estimates.

1   See, for example, the KMPG administrative burdens exercise for the UK's HM Revenue and Customs, available at http://www.hmrc.gov.uk/better-regulation/kpmg.htm, last accessed 21 August 2008.

Tax compliance has, until the advent of computers, largely been conducted through labour-intensive manual paper-based systems. The role of the revenue authorities has also been instrumental in the structure, reporting and audit requirements of these systems, particularly in the UK, where different agencies with differing powers have been responsible for setting tax policy and collection of different taxes.

The history of the hidden costs of taxation is therefore influenced by a number of factors: the numbers of taxpayers, the structure of the tax system and the legislative response by national governments to protect revenue streams from avoidance, evasion and international tax competition. Costs are also influenced by advances in technology and communications that aid tax compliance and developments in research that improve understanding of the scope of the hidden costs of taxation. This chapter will review each of these areas.

Numbers of taxpayers and structure

In a historical context the vast majority of the population has been subject to some form of taxation throughout the ages, be it directly or indirectly. In medieval times landowners would be required to pay taxes on land that were in turn paid for by tenants. In the early eighteenth century it was estimated that the poor paid almost half of their income in forms of indirect taxation (Lymer and Oats, 2008). The nature of compliance costs, however, comes from the requirement of the taxpayer to meet their own obligation to pay tax. For most taxpayers this tax is Income Tax. As stated above, Income Tax was paid by fewer than one million people at the turn of the twentieth century; this number reached almost

32 million in 2006/07, however.[2] The number of taxes has also increased, so that the tax system now captures a broader base of economic activities, and this has increased the number of taxes with which taxpayers must comply. The trend in the increasing number of taxes impacting upon businesses is evident with the recent introductions of the aggregates levy, climate change levy, landfill tax, VAT and air passenger duty.

In the case of Income Tax in the UK, the tax had an intermittent introduction until it became a permanent feature in 1842, introduced by the then prime minister, Robert Peel. The justification for the reintroduction of the Income Tax in 1842 used by Peel during his speech to Parliament perhaps gives an insight into why Income Tax is now paid by so many people and why other forms of taxation are used to collect revenues for state use.

> I propose that the income of the country should bear a charge not exceeding seven pence in the pound, for the purpose of not only supplying the deficiency in the revenue, but of enabling me with confidence and satisfaction to propose great commercial reforms, which will afford a hope of reviving commerce, and such an improvement in the manufacturing interests as will react on every interest in the country, and by diminishing the prices of articles of consumption and the cost of living, will, in a pecuniary point of view, compensate you for your present sacrifices, whilst you will be, at the same time, relieved from the contemplation of a great public evil. (See Blunden, 1892: 638)

By use of the phrase 'on every interest in the country' Peel

---

2   Latest confirmed figures at the time of writing. See HMRC statistics, Table 1.4, available at http://www.hmrc.gov.uk/stats/tax_receipts/menu.htm, last accessed 9 June 2009.

appears to link taxation to the benefits that people derive from paying the tax. Indeed, since Peel's time the UK state has become increasingly involved in the provision of services to the population. Taxation is the method used by government to raise funds for public services but also to influence behaviours (such as duties placed on alcohol and tobacco and on air flights), and to redistribute income and wealth (Nellis and Parker, 1996).

It is widely accepted that the imposition of some level of taxes on a population is a necessity, and typically where there is support for government policies, compliance with taxation is high (Erard and Feinstein, 1994). Negative responses, such as tax avoidance and evasion, that are damaging to government's revenue-raising measures are not always widespread, and often when the origin and purpose of the tax requirement are known and understood, citizens may approve of such policies, thus leading to low levels of tax avoidance and evasion (Lewis, 1982; Erard and Feinstein, 1994).

As tax systems have developed and the provision of services by the state has increased, greater burdens have been placed on taxpayers, first in terms of the reporting and record-keeping that are required to prevent under-reporting and evasion of taxes, but also in terms of the requirement for the state to tax activities that had not previously been taxed.

Overview of research into the hidden costs of taxation

The first studies into the level of compliance costs incurred by taxpayers were undertaken by Haig (1935) in the USA. Sandford et al. (1989) note that until this time economists had generally dismissed measurement of the compliance cost burden on taxpayers in favour of studying what were considered to be the more important of Smith's Canons of Taxation: equity and efficiency. Tran-Nam et al. (2000) consider this neglect in the literature to be due to the belief that compliance costs were insignificant, there was no formal model to reduce compliance costs, and the research required to determine these costs is *'painstaking'* (p. 230).

Haig's work concluded that there is a trade-off between administration costs and compliance costs. What is perhaps interesting is that this is still very much a part of the debate today, and in a report produced as part of the Mirrlees Review of the UK tax system led by the Institute for Fiscal Studies, Shaw et al. (2008) note that it is preferable for HMRC to have employees' taxes collected and paid by their employer, although this in turn creates a cost burden on the employer in meeting that obligation. One of the main reasons for this is that the revenue authority would have to deal with a considerable number of reluctant taxpayers if the tax were not collected by the employer, and the cost of collection would be expected to rise considerably.

Haig's work is followed by that of Martin (1944), although there were criticisms of this early work in that it did not identify the costly areas of compliance, just producing an overall total. Subsequent to this a number of studies focus on different forms of tax, such as Yocum (1961), which considers Sales Tax compliance. The significant finding of that piece of research was that the cost of Sales Tax collection as a percentage of tax liability is generally greater for small stores. Müller (1963) confirms this conclusion in a study of small businesses and notes that the costs associated with tax are disproportionately higher for small firms. Müller also recognises the costs incurred as a result of business owners' record-keeping and use of accountants hired for the purposes of tax compliance. He concluded that this extra expense was incurred in part as a result of anxiety caused by the tax system in meeting the legal obligations imposed by the tax authorities.

Sandford et al. (1989: 30) summarise the key messages and findings from the early North American research into tax compliance costs that feature in the research today.

1) Compliance costs are not directly proportional to liability or taxable income.
2) Compliance costs are regressive; economies of scale are likely to occur.
3) Compliance costs are related to occupation; the self-employed incur high costs.
4) Compliance costs are variable, and are especially likely to increase when taxable activities cannot be predicted and made routine.
5) Multi-state operation is associated with high costs, especially where the states use different definitions of the tax base and of tax borderlines.
6) Ceteris paribus, sales tax costs also vary with the number of transactions undertaken.
7) Costs of change will be high.
8) Costs of operating low-yield taxes are high (in ratio terms).
9) There may be scope for trade-offs between taxpayer compliance costs and administrative costs.

In both the USA and Canada it was not until the 1980s that the next studies into compliance costs took place. US research again focused on Sales Tax and was undertaken by Peat Marwick (1985), although Pitt and Slemrod (1988) published findings of their research into the compliance cost burden of itemising deductions for Income Tax. Sales taxes also featured as part of an unpublished federal government study in Canada during the 1980s (Sandford et al., 1989), and Vaillancourt (1989) investigated personal income and payroll taxes, finding that they are more burdensome for smaller firms operating payroll deduction systems, and these burdens decrease as a proportion of total business income as firm size increases.

In Europe the earliest example of a study into tax compliance cost burdens is that of Strümpel (1966). Although limited to small business owners, Strümpel's study finds that compliance costs are regressive, particularly so for the self-employed in West Germany at that time, who he states are *'forced'* (p. 74) to spend considerable amounts of their own time in compliance activities. Also in this is discussion of the negative psychological nature of the taxpayer's response to compliance activities. Strümpel frames his argument within Smith's canon of equity: '[the compliance cost burden] is basically regressive ... [and] inconsistent with the goals of progressive income taxation' (p. 75). Johnson (1990) uses equity and efficiency arguments to suggest that small firms deserve preferential tax treatment, although Holtz-Eakin (1995, 2000) dismisses the preferential treatment of small firms on the grounds that the tax system is an inappropriate means of compensating such businesses for the structural disadvantages that they face. Although both authors recognise the benefit of economies of scale to larger firms and the regressive nature of regulation on smaller firms, neither specifically refers to compliance costs associated with the tax regime, despite the growing literature in this area.

As Bannock (2005) notes, the dearth of literature on the nature of compliance costs, and the wider regulatory burden of government legislation, can be demonstrated by the scant attention given to these issues in the Bolton Report in 1971 (Bolton, 1971); although the proposed introduction of VAT is discussed owing to the anticipated high costs for small firms. Despite this absence at the time of the Bolton Report's publication, a research programme was already under way at the University of Bath's Centre for Fiscal Studies, led by Cedric Sandford.

The work by Sandford and his colleagues is discussed below; this research programme spawned a great interest in the area of compliance costs, however, including studies conducted by Pope et al. (e.g. 1991) in Australia. Pope et al.'s work was the only study in that country at the time. The Australian Tax Office refuted the level of the compliance costs estimated in the research and conducted its own study. The resulting publications, ATAX (1997) and Walpole et al. (1999), confirmed, however, that compliance costs are regressive in nature and fall most heavily on small firms.

A number of countries, particularly in the OECD, have engaged in compliance costs research (Tran-Nam et al. 2000). Sandford (1995: 411) suggests: 'Governments concerned with the health of the economy must have a concern for the level of compliance costs and an objective to reduce them.' Recognising the importance of compliance costs, many countries introduced compliance cost assessments to accompany changes to regulatory burdens on businesses; the Netherlands and the UK introduced these measures in 1985.

Sandford's research into tax compliance costs

Sandford's research into the compliance costs associated with taxation marked a major new step. His 1973 publication was based on earlier research as part of a programme at the University of Bath's Centre for Fiscal Studies and reproduced substantial elements of two previous publications. The research surveyed personal taxpayers and professional tax advisers (accountants), along with a study of letters to press inquiry bureaux and queries to Citizens Advice Bureaux. The study reported seven main conclusions:

1. The main measurable compliance costs were the sums paid to advisers, the value of the taxpayer's time and those of operating PAYE.
2. Compliance costs in respect of fees for advisers and the time of unpaid tax advisers rose sharply in the period 1965–70.
3. High compliance costs were incurred mainly by the self-employed and those on low incomes, with 90 per cent of the self-employed surveyed paying for tax advice.
4. At the time a substantial proportion of the requests to organisations such as the Citizens Advice Bureau relating to tax were from those retiring and from women changing marital status, yet these groups typically had very low levels of income.
5. Capital Gains Tax was identified as a tax with high compliance costs as it was complicated, confusing and horizontally inequitable.
6. Tax avoidance itself leads to costs: the resources used to devise and implement avoidance schemes, the distortion caused by business implementing such schemes, and the psychological costs.
7. There are widespread difficulties in understanding the tax system that hamper communication between the revenue authorities and the taxpayer.

Sandford's findings are consistent with earlier examples of research into compliance costs from around the world, and his work continued well into the 1990s. Given the imminent introduction of a Sales Tax in the UK in 1973 it is hardly surprising that the next substantial contribution from Sandford's research programme concerned the costs and benefits of VAT (Sandford et al. 1981).

The Sandford et al. (ibid.) study into the costs and benefits of VAT not only presents research into the compliance costs associated with a particular form of taxation, it is the first example in the literature that considers the benefits to the business of compliance with the tax system, and therefore presents net compliance costs. In particular the authors investigate the cash-flow benefits to the business of collecting and retaining tax before it must be paid over to the tax authorities, as well as the non-pecuniary benefits to the business of better record-keeping, such as improved stock control. In terms of the cash-flow benefits, Sandford et al. (ibid.) observe that cash-flow benefits almost wipe out the compliance costs associated with VAT for the largest of firms, whereas the cash-flow benefits remain modest for small firms in relation to costs. Small firms, however, were considered to be the beneficiaries of the non-pecuniary benefits of VAT compliance, such as improved record-keeping.

The principal finding of the 1981 study into the costs and benefits of VAT was that businesses as a whole in the UK were burdened with £392 million (equivalent to £1.624 billion in 2006/07) in measurable compliance costs during 1977/78, and the taxpayer was also funding the £85 million (equivalent to £352 million in 2006/07) administrative costs of HM Customs and Excise related to the VAT system. Expressed as a proportion of taxable turnover, the authors found that traders with turnover up to £20,000 had compliance costs some thirty to forty times greater than those of firms with taxable turnover of more than £1 million, making these costs highly regressive. Table 9 highlights the regressive nature of VAT compliance by reporting the findings of Sandford et al. (ibid.).

Table 9 **Compliance costs for VAT as a proportion of taxable turnover, 1977/78**

Taxable turnover (£ thousands p.a.)	Compliance costs as a percentage of taxable turnover (mean)
0–9.9	1.64
10–19.9	1.23
20–49.9	0.74
50–99.9	0.54
100–999.9	0.24
1,000 and over	0.04
Overall weighted mean	0.92

Source: Sandford et al. (1989)

In 1989 Sandford et al. brought together into one publication the most comprehensive study of compliance costs of one nation's tax system. Sandford et al.'s 1989 book *Administrative and Compliance Costs of Taxation* was written with considerable cooperation from the then two tax revenue authorities in the UK: Inland Revenue and HM Customs and Excise (HMCE). The list of taxes and duties is long, though of most interest in this monograph are those associated with PAYE/NIC collection by employers, Corporation Tax compliance, VAT and personal Income Tax.

The burden placed on employers as a result of operating PAYE to collect and pay employees' Income Tax and National Insurance payments was estimated to be £449 million in 1981/82 (equivalent to £1.145 billion in 2006/07). As in the VAT compliance study conducted earlier (Sandford et al. 1981), the authors found that there were cash-flow benefits associated with this form of tax compliance. It was also found that compliance costs are regressive and in the case of the largest firms net compliance costs are negative owing to the cash-flow benefit to the organisation from the taxes collected. The regressive nature of PAYE/NIC compliance costs can be seen in Table 10. An international comparison was also conducted with two studies, one in Ireland and one in Canada, finding similar regressive traits in these elements of the two respective tax regimes.

Table 10 **Compliance costs for PAYE/NICs per employee, 1981/82**

Number of employees	Mean compliance cost per employee (£)
1–5	58
6–10	39
11–20	38
21–50	29
51–100	17
101–500	18
Over 500	11

Source: Sandford et al. (1989)

For VAT compliance, in the 1989 publication, Sandford et al. draw upon their earlier study and a second study carried out in 1986/87. In the intervening period they found that compliance costs for VAT appeared to have fallen in real terms. Compliance costs in 1986/87 were estimated to be some £791 million (equivalent to £1.605 billion in 2006/07) and retained their regressive nature. The reduction in compliance costs was mainly due to the abolition of the higher rate of VAT and simplification measures introduced by HM Customs and Excise, such as permission to electronically submit invoice information and changes to inspection visits for small firms. Electronic submission is clearly important to reducing compliance costs, and here the impact is observed for the first time in the UK. The authors have some words of caution, however. Given that simplification measures were being put in place, the reduction in compliance costs was happening at a time when underlying costs were increasing owing to the use of accountants for VAT work. The increased costs associated with VAT in the UK were reinforced by the level of negative attitudes towards VAT.

The element of the study (ibid.) associated with Corporation Tax compliance was based on semi-structured interviews. When the data for compliance costs is disaggregated into size of company by employment or turnover, the sample sizes become small. There is also difficulty for the authors in determining total compliance cost for Corporation Tax at the level of the economy owing to inadequate national statistics on the number of companies. Despite these drawbacks the total compliance cost burden on companies in 1986/87 was estimated to be £300 million (equivalent to £609 million in 2006/07). Once again compliance costs are found to be regressive based on employment size, as shown in Table 11.

An international comparison was not possible for Corporation Tax owing to the absence of international studies at the time. A study conducted in 2001 and reported in Kauser et al. (2005),

Table 11 **Compliance costs for Corporation Tax as a percentage of taxable turnover analysed by size of company, 1986/87**

Size of company by no. of employees	Compliance costs as percentage of taxable turnover
1–5	0.48
6–10	0.19
11–25	0.09
26–50	0.05
51–100	0.07
100–500	0.02
Over 500	0.01

Source: Sandford et al. (1989)

however, found that Corporation Tax compliance costs, though regressive, were not as bad for smaller companies as the Sandford et al. (1989) findings. Kauser et al. estimated that total Corporation Tax compliance costs at the level of the economy were some £608 million (equivalent to £725 million in 2006/07). A comparison of the distribution of the compliance cost burden estimated by both studies is shown in Table 12.

Table 12 **Corporation Tax compliance costs as a percentage of taxable turnover**

Taxable turnover (£)	Sandford et al. (1989)	Kauser et al. (2005)
0–100,000	0.97	0.31
100,001–500,000	0.17	0.24
500,001–1,000,000	0.07	0.13
1,000,001–10,000,000	0.03	0.11
10,000,000 and over	0.01	0.04

Sources: Sandford et al. (1989); Kauser et al. (2005)

Finally personal Income Tax is of particular importance, as this is the means by which most of the self-employed are assessed for Income Tax. The self-employed are Schedule D taxpayers in the UK. Schedule E taxpayers are employees and tend to have simple affairs, and virtually all their tax is deducted by their employer as PAYE/NIC; therefore, as one might have assumed, the cost of compliance falls more heavily on the self-employed and, as Table 13 confirms, these costs are regressive. The self-employed are able to defer payment of the tax, unlike employees, and the authors therefore estimated that the net compliance costs for the self-employed were £680 million (equivalent to £811 million in 2006/07) after allowing for a significant £122 million cash-flow benefit (equivalent to £146 million in 2006/07).

Table 13 **Comparison of average compliance costs of Schedule D and E taxpayers, 1983/84**

Income band (£)	Schedule D (self-employed)		Schedule E (employed)	
	Mean compliance cost (£)	As percentage of income	Mean compliance cost (£)	As percentage of income
Up to 7,499	274	6.79	1	0.13
7,500–14,999	411	3.87	122	1.06
15,000–29,999	618	2.93	182	0.85
30,000–49,999	513	1.49	606	1.51
50,000 and over	1,397	1.65	607	0.83

Source: Sandford et al. (1989: 74)

Developments in the study of payroll compliance cost burdens

In 1995 the Inland Revenue and the Department of Social Security commissioned the Centre for Fiscal Studies at the University of Bath to undertake a detailed examination of the compliance cost burden to employers of operating PAYE, expenses and benefits in kind, National Insurance, Statutory Sick Pay and Statutory Maternity Pay in the UK (Inland Revenue, 1998). This report is often referred to as the 'Bath Report'. Despite retaining links with the University of Bath, Cedric Sandford was not directly involved in this particular compliance cost project.

The Bath Report's main finding was that total payroll compliance costs for employers in 1995/96 amounted to £1.32 billion (equivalent to £1.79 billion in 2006/07), and compared with the earlier study conducted and reported by Sandford et al. (1989), it was the opinion of the authors that this figure was an increase of 42 per cent and of the same order as the growth in UK GDP over the period. Not surprisingly the study found these compliance costs to be highly regressive, with some 75 per cent of the costs being incurred by the smallest 30 per cent of employers and the cash-flow benefits to those employing more than a thousand people being greater than the compliance costs.

The report makes two further important contributions. First, the average marginal compliance cost of an employee was found to be £14 per annum – though this figure was much higher for the smallest firms and lower for larger. For a new starter the compliance cost figure rose to £73. The second contribution is that, for the first time, it examined the cost effectiveness of what were then new payroll technologies.

Two studies by the Small Business Research Trust into the

compliance costs associated with payroll activities in the UK (SBRT, 1996, 1998) found that, based on business owners' perceptions of compliance costs as a percentage of turnover, compliance costs were higher than those found in the Bath Report. The difference in the research methods does not provide a suitable comparison between the two sets of research; Chittenden et al. (2005), however, based on research conducted in 2001/02, provides a useful insight into the trends in compliance costs and the reasons for the differences between the SBRT research and the Bath Report's findings. In this research the authors measure the additive[3] compliance costs and compare these with the outcomes from the Bath Study. Table 14 highlights the similarity in the outcomes of the Bath Report (Inland Revenue, 1998) and Chittenden et al. (2005).

Chittenden et al. (2005) used the outcome of their research and the Manchester Business School Small and Medium Sized Business Tax Model to estimate that incorporated businesses employing up to a hundred people and unincorporated firms employing up to twenty people in the UK incurred compliance costs associated with payroll activities of £1.12 billion in 2001/02 (equivalent to £1.31 billion in 2006/07). Their study also included questions relating to attitudes towards payroll burdens. Their findings show that 85.6 per cent of respondents felt that

3   In the most recent study by the University of Bath (Inland Revenue, 1998) compliance costs for PAYE and NIC were measured both in actual terms, what they term 'additive costs', and in terms of perceived costs, what they term 'reported costs'. Interestingly, and contrary to expectations, in some size bands, 'additive costs' (actual or measured costs) are lower than 'reported costs' (perceived costs); while in other size bands the opposite is true. Compliance costs based on additive costs (measured costs) include the value of time spent in compliance by proprietors, qualified accounting staff and other staff as well as fees paid to professional advisers and other costs (such as computing and stationery costs).

Table 14 **Comparison of Bath Report outcomes and Chittenden et al. (2005) for payroll compliance costs**

Bath Report (Inland Revenue, 1998) Data from 1995/96		Chittenden et al. (2005) Data from 2001/02	
No. of employees	Compliance costs, 2001, £ per employee (2006/07 prices)	No. of employees	Compliance costs, 2001, £ per employee (2006/07 prices)
1–4	308 (367)	1–4	335 (400)
5–9	153 (182)	5–9	170 (203)
10–49	95 (113)	10–49	123 (147)
50–99	62 (74)	50–99	56 (67)
100–499	44 (52)	100 and over	21 (25)
500–999	31 (37)		
1,000–4,999	31 (37)		
5,000 and over	5 (6)		

Source: Chittenden et al. (2005)

the increasing complexity of the PAYE/NIC system in the UK caused by Working Families' Tax Credits, Statutory Sick Pay and Statutory Maternity Pay were disadvantages of operating this system. The authors conclude that, despite the UK tax authority's attempts to reduce compliance costs associated with payroll activities, changes and increasing complexity were inhibiting real reductions.

In an international context, as part of an ongoing programme of tax compliance studies by ATAX at the University of New South Wales, Tran-Nam et al. (2000) report that PAYE compliance costs in Australia amount to 1.3 per cent of the taxes collected. This finding is in line with Sandford et al. (1989: 95), who find that in the UK the cost of compliance is 'just over 1% of the yield'. Tran-Nam et al. also note in their conclusions that given the regressive nature of compliance costs, their redistribution is one of the biggest policy challenges for the Australian tax authorities and those around the world; their findings for PAYE in Australia also showed that for the very largest of companies there is a positive monetary benefit from operating payroll, whereas the largest burden falls on the very smallest of employers.

Developments in the study of Sales Tax compliance costs

As indicated earlier in this chapter, much of the earliest literature, and Sandford's first substantial contribution in the area of compliance costs, has been devoted to Sales Tax, Retail Tax or VAT in the UK. Numerous studies into VAT systems have been conducted around the world, including in Germany, Sweden, Canada, New Zealand and the Netherlands (Hansford et al. 2003). These studies share many similarities in their findings: the regressive nature of compliance costs, economies of scale for larger firms, and cash-flow benefits for larger firms. Hansford et al. go on to determine the influence of a number of factors on VAT compliance costs using a multiple regression model and find, as expected, that they are regressive.

Such is the regressive nature of VAT compliance costs that Chittenden et al. (1999a, 1999b) have suggested that the VAT registration threshold in the UK is a barrier to growth for smaller firms. In this research it was proposed that the VAT registration limit should be lifted to £250,000, although the introduction of a £100,000 threshold would have reduced VAT compliance costs at the time by £0.6 billion. Evidence that VAT compliance is a barrier to growth is provided by Kauser et al. (2001), who find

Table 15 **Comparison of VAT compliance cost studies**

Sandford et al. (1989)		SBRT (1998)		Kauser et al. (2001)		
Turnover	%	Turnover	%	Turnover	%*	%†
£0–20,499	1.94	£0–£20,000	1.58	£0–£20,499	0.24	1.52
£20,500–£49,999	0.78	£20,000–£49,999	2.22	£20,500–£49,999	0.18	2.17
£50,000–£99,999	0.52	£50,000–£149,999	2.93	£50,000–£99,999	0.15	1.91
£100,000–£499,999	0.42	£150,000–£349,999	2.48	£100,000–£499,999	0.11	1.15
£500,000–£999,999	0.26	£350,000–£749,999	1.66	£500,000–£999,999	0.07	0.45
£1,000,000–£9,999,999	0.04	£750,000–£1,499,999	0.90	£1,000,000–£9,999,999	0.02	0.20
£10,000,000 +	0.03	£1,500,000 +	1.23	£10,000,000 +	0.11	0.22
All	0.69	All	2.07	All	0.12	1.09

NB: The turnover bands used in the SBRT study are different, as shown below.

* Additive compliance costs.

† Reported compliance costs.

that some business owners manage their turnover to avoid VAT registration; Hansford et al. (2003) complement this by demonstrating that the psychological costs of VAT compliance are a major factor leading to the perception of high compliance costs among small businesses.

Kauser et al. (2001) measure additive and reported compliance costs in their study and compare and contrast these with the earlier study by Sandford et al. (1989) and a study by the Small Business Research Trust (SBRT, 1998).[4] The first column of the Kauser et al. results shows the additive compliance costs results and the second shows the reported or perceived costs. While the

---

4   The SBRT research in this case is the same as that referred to in the PAYE section
     and measures reported costs.

authors caution against direct comparison between the studies, this appears to demonstrate that total compliance costs of VAT have fallen since the Sandford et al. (1989) study, although the perceived costs are somewhat similar to those found by the SBRT study. These figures are shown in Table 15.

Concluding remarks

Despite the identification of a cost obligation other than the incidence of a tax itself by Adam Smith, research into compliance costs, or the hidden costs of taxation, had been neglected until the mid-to-late twentieth century. With few notable exceptions it was not until the work of Sandford (1973) that research in this field gained momentum.

The hidden costs of taxation have become increasingly of concern as governments around the world introduce new means of taxation to attempt to ensure equity and efficiency in their tax systems and further seek to enhance the amount of tax collected to pay for greater public service provision and to influence behaviours and the performance of their respective economies. Costs have increased as more people and businesses are captured by, and must comply with, tax legislation; and the number of taxes with which these taxpayers must comply has increased over the years. Governments now rely more heavily on businesses to operate as tax collectors and payers on their behalf, however, often with an increased burden on the business which incurs costs.

It seems to have been accepted that, for most taxes, collection by and payment by businesses is a more efficient means of tax gathering. Administrative costs of collecting taxes would be much higher if revenue authorities had to deal with millions of taxpayers separately, increasing the costs of collection and verification of liability which in turn would lead to a greater tax burden to meet the extra costs.

The costs to businesses of compliance with taxation are not, however, distributed in an equitable manner and fall most heavily on those smaller businesses that perhaps are least able to cope with these costs. The use of technology has become more widespread and much cheaper for these businesses; they still face a considerable disadvantage, however, compared with the largest companies, which often gain a net revenue benefit from tax compliance. Table 8, derived in Chapter 2, and based on the latest compliance cost work, clearly demonstrates the regressive nature of tax administration costs. This showed that the smallest firms paid sixteen times the proportion of turnover in tax compliance costs that large firms paid. The detailed work on individual taxes that has been discussed in this chapter has not been repeated recently. The aggregate estimates derived in Chapter 2, however, are entirely consistent with the earlier detailed work on individual taxes discussed in this chapter.

The issue of compliance costs for smaller firms has been a challenge that many governments, including that of the UK, have been attempting to address. Despite the recognition of the burdens on businesses and attempts to reduce these, however, governments have continued to introduce complexity and additional reporting and compliance activities that have maintained these costs and their regressive nature.

In the following chapter, more recent research will be examined that considers moves to reduce compliance cost burdens, including further developments in the use of technology to reduce costs for revenue authorities and the taxpayer, along with governments' attempts to measure the burden of compliance and set targets for their reduction.

4 RECENT DEVELOPMENTS IN THE ECONOMIC CONTEXT OF TAX COMPLIANCE COSTS

This chapter reviews the changing environment in which tax policy operates and how this relates to the hidden costs of taxation. We also consider international trends in the measurement of administrative burdens, the methods used to accomplish this, and the setting of targets to achieve a reduction in this burden.

In recent years there have been a number of changes in advanced economies which are altering the landscape relating to the hidden costs of taxation. As discussed in previous chapters, government became used to relying on businesses to administer systems on their behalf. In the UK, Shaw et al. (2008: 27) calculate that approximately 88 per cent of all tax revenue is remitted by businesses (based on HMRC figures for 2006/07). Given the regressive nature of compliance costs, however, the loading of regulation on to business is likely to become increasingly unpopular.

In his former role as Chancellor of the Exchequer, Gordon Brown said: 'It is essential that tax policy is based on clear principles. These are to encourage work, savings and investment, and fairness. Fairness by ensuring that everyone bears their fair share of taxation and pays the correct amount and which is seen to be fair by vigorous pursuit of tax avoidance and evasion' (Financial Statement and Budget Report (FSBR), July 1997; see Hurwich, 2001).

Clearly, it is at least arguable that the regressive nature of -compliance costs is 'unfair'.

Additionally there have been a number of changes in society and the economy which may result in the use of businesses to collect taxes becoming less effective in the future.

Changes in the composition of the workforce in the UK

The PAYE system delivers approximately 30 per cent of government revenues (Whiting, 2003: 11) and has worked reasonably well for a majority of employees in times of more or less stable employment. On the other hand, Shaw et al. (2008: 38) note that 'Although in some ways PAYE has proved to be adaptable, there have been complaints over a number of decades that it lacks flexibility and therefore constrains tax policy.'

The employment environment has been changing. In recent years, sometimes as result of economic conditions, and sometimes in response to increasing regulation (tax-related and otherwise – see below), the composition of the workforce has altered substantially.

Generally, employment is now more varied: individuals change jobs more frequently, there are more part-time and temporary jobs, and individuals may have multiple sources of income. There has been significant growth in the numbers of self-employed individuals and a growth in smaller firms, and (as the trend for portfolio working becomes more popular) the tendency for individuals to have more than one job. An indication of the magnitude of the issue is given below.

In 2006, there were an estimated 4.5 million private sector businesses in the UK, of which over 99 per cent were firms with fewer than 50 employees and 96 per cent were firms with fewer than ten employees (referred to as micro-businesses). Most businesses in the UK have no employees (other than the owner in the case of incorporated firms). The number of businesses with no employees increased from just over 2.5 million (68 per cent) in 1996, to over 3 million (73 per cent) in 2006. By contrast, the number of businesses with at least one employee did not rise at all between 1996 and 2006, thus falling as a percentage of the total to just over 25 per cent. A disproportionate amount of the increase in the number of businesses in recent years has been of businesses with no employees.

Factors leading to growth in self-employment

Table 16 shows the growth over the twelve years to 2007 in the numbers of self-employed people who do not employ others, including both incorporated and unincorporated businesses. This growth in self-employment accounts for virtually all of the increase in the stock of UK businesses over this period.

Table 16 **Total number of micro firms in UK economy by number of employees, 1996 and 2007**

	0 employees	1–4 employees	5–9 employees	Total micro firms
1996	2,516,819	812,971	197,133	3,526,923
	71.36%	23.05%	5.59%	100%
2007	3,468,100	858,245	221,600	4,547,945
	76.26%	18.87%	4.87%	100%

Source: SBS Statistics, now found at http://stats.berr.gov.uk/ed/sme/, accessed 2 June 2009

Self-employment and the costs of tax compliance

The increased attractiveness of self-employment[1] compared with employee status (both for employer and employee) has come about at least in part owing to increases in the cost of National Insurance Contributions and also to more onerous employment legislation. Redston (2004) has noted that there exists a trade-off between earnings and employment rights that has resulted in an increase in self-employment despite the presence of tax rules to prevent businesses passing off employment as self-employment. Redston argues, with support of evidence from the SBS Annual Survey 2003, that there is resistance to employing individuals owing to tax and employment regulations, leading to the lack of an incentive for individuals and businesses to engage in an employee/employer arrangement. The favourable position of the self-employed and the disincentive for a business to employ result in a situation where both businesses and the self-employed can mutually benefit from cost savings. The potential employer pays more for labour, without the risks of employment law but gaining added flexibility, and the self-employed person trades off their employment rights for increased financial rewards. The cost of tax compliance is one aspect of this total regulatory burden borne by employer businesses.

Problems caused by artificially induced self-employment

One of the problems of artificially induced self-employment is that it affects tax revenue. From a taxation perspective, self-employment almost certainly results in a lower tax take to the Exchequer because of:

---

1   Trading either as a limited company or as an unincorporated business.

- Lower rates of National Insurance Contributions compared with those paid by employees.
- Lower Income Tax because of the more flexible treatment of business expenses.
- Lower Income Tax and National Insurance revenue because of the greater opportunities for under-reporting of income available to 'own-account' workers. In a study of US tax amnesty participants, Young (1994) finds that 84 per cent of those taxpayers with the ability to evade taxes will do so to some extent. Young specifically identifies the self-employed as those with the greatest opportunity to under-report income. Though this is an old study and originated in the USA, there is no reason to suppose that these problems do not exist in the UK.
- There is also a cash-flow change on becoming self-employed as tax payments are made in arrears in January and July each year compared with monthly for employees.

Given the discussion in earlier chapters concerning the regressivity of compliance costs (the higher burden borne by smaller firms), it seems reasonable to suggest that an increase in the numbers of small firms will result in overall increases in the hidden costs of taxation.

The relatively short lives of most small firms is another complicating factor leading to a rise in the aggregate costs of setting up and closing businesses and the associated tax administration. The costs associated with start-up and cessation tend to be fixed in nature and therefore these compliance costs are difficult to reduce.

World Bank *Doing Business* initiative

Since the 1970s there has been an increase in awareness in Europe and the USA of the impact of regulations on business. These are generally referred to as Administrative Burdens (AB), of which the costs of complying with the tax regime are a part. There are two initiatives that may have a restraining effect on the growth in tax compliance costs: first, the World Bank *Doing Business* initiative, and second, the Administrative Burdens Reduction Exercise (see below).

The World Bank began a multi-year project to measure the 'ease of doing business' by developing an index of business regulation for (initially) 130 countries based on actual regulations such as the number of procedures and the time and costs needed to register a new business. The first report was issued in 2003 and focused on five regulatory aspects: starting a business, hiring and firing workers, enforcing contracts, getting credit and closing a business. In later years the number of topics examined has been expanded. The conclusions from the 2003 report were that: i) regulation varies widely around the world, ii) heavier regulation of business activity generally brings adverse economic outcomes, while clearly defined and well-protected property rights enhance prosperity, and iii) rich countries regulate business in a consistent manner, poor countries do not. An important finding from this study is that countries with a less regulated business environment have realised higher productivity (World Bank, 2003).

Later World Bank studies (2006 onwards) examine the ease of paying taxes in each country. World Bank (2006) acknowledges that there are good ways and bad ways to collect taxes. It assesses the burden of tax compliance across the participating countries and identifies a number of issues contributing to this.

These include: the number of taxes a business is subject to; the number of tax payments required to be made; the number of tax agencies dealt with; and the hours taken to comply with tax requirements. The study argues against the emphasis on tax rates, particularly corporate Income Tax rates, usually found in lobbying for Business Tax reform, claiming that for the majority of countries corporate Income Taxes represent a small share of the total business tax burden (less than 25 per cent on average). Additionally it cites the complexity of tax compliance as important (particularly the number of interactions with the tax authorities), reporting survey responses which indicate that in several countries working with the tax bureaucracy is considered a bigger problem than tax rates themselves. In fact, as the study reports, 'Firms in 90% of surveyed countries rank tax administration among the top 5 obstacles to doing business.' Bearing in mind the discussion in previous chapters, we can see that these factors contribute to both the financial and the psychic costs of compliance.

Doing Business 2006: *ease of paying taxes methodology*

In order to assess which countries make paying taxes easy, *Doing Business* asked accountants in 155 countries to review the financial statements and a list of transactions of a standardised firm called TaxpayerCo.[2] The business started with the same financial position in every country. Respondents were asked the total tax that the business must pay and the process for doing so. All taxes

---

2   The survey was conducted in partnership with PricewaterhouseCoopers, using a methodology developed in an ongoing research project by Mihir Desai, Caralee McLiesh, Rita Ramalho and Andrei Shleifer (PwC, 2007).

– from corporate Income Tax to VAT, to advertising and environmental taxes – and all applicable deductions and exemptions are taken into account to calculate the total burden.[3]

Administrative requirements are a serious burden in many countries. *Doing Business* measures the number of payments TaxpayerCo would have to make to tax authorities, as well as the time required to prepare and file tax payments. In 2006 the report noted that it takes 84 payments and 2,185 hours a year in Ukraine, but only 11 payments and 104 hours in Estonia.

Rankings for the ease of paying taxes are calculated as the average of the country rankings for total taxes, number of payments and time required to comply. The 2006 study found that Middle Eastern and East Asian countries make paying taxes the easiest. Latin American countries impose the heaviest burdens, mainly because of compliance costs. Africa follows, largely because of high taxes. OECD countries impose the smallest administrative burdens and charge moderate tax bills.

The 2006 report found that rich countries tend to have lower business taxes and make them less complex. Simple, moderate taxes and fast, cheap administration mean less hassle for business – as well as higher revenues. In contrast, poor countries tend to use business as a collection point, charging higher business taxes. 'Such burdensome taxes create incentives for evasion. In the United States business taxes add up to 21% of gross profit. So if a company started with $100 in gross profit, evading 20% of its tax bill would raise gross profit after tax from $79 to $83 – equivalent

---

3   A common method for assessing tax rates is the marginal effective tax rate (METR) method, which estimates the tax payable resulting from investing one more unit of capital, or hiring one more worker, or producing one more unit of output. See the Data notes in *Doing Business* 2006 for a description of the main differences between the METR and *Doing Business* methods.

to increasing gross profit by 5%. But in Mauritania profit would jump 63%' (World Bank, 2005: 47).

Doing Business 2006 set the ball rolling with the thorny issue of tax reform, recognising that '... both business and government benefit when taxes are simple and fair and set incentives for growth'.

It suggests four possible reforms to begin with:

- Consolidate the number of taxes – because having more types of taxes requires more interaction between businesses and tax agencies and increases compliance costs.
- Cut back special exemptions and privileges – these contribute to complexity and lack of transparency and make the tax system costly to run, thus increasing administrative costs.
- Simplify filing requirements, for example by electronic filing and the simplification of paper filing; the UK, for example, shortened its VAT return to one page.
- Broaden the tax base by keeping rates moderate in developing countries – it is suggested that keeping tax rates moderate will encourage compliance and consequently may increase tax revenues. The study found evidence that, especially in poor countries, higher rates of taxation tend to push businesses into the informal economy and as a result the tax base decreases and less revenue is collected.

From 2007 onwards *Doing Business* publishes an 'ease of paying taxes' composite ranking for each country based on the number of tax payments, time to prepare and file tax returns and to pay taxes, and total taxes as a share of profit before all taxes borne. A selection of the results is shown in Table 17.

Table 17 **Where is it easy to pay taxes – and where not?**

Easiest	Rank	Most difficult	Rank
Maldives	1	Panama	172
Qatar	2	Jamaica	173
Hong Kong, China	3	Mauritania	174
United Arab Emirates	4	Gambia, The	175
Singapore	5	Bolivia	176
Ireland	6	Venezuela	177
Saudi Arabia	7	Central African Republic	178
Oman	8	Congo, Rep.	179
Kuwait	9	Ukraine	180
Kiribati	10	Belarus	181

Source: World Bank (2009: Table 8.1)

In the full table, the UK is ranked 16th in 2009, and the USA 46th.

A further motivation for countries to reform is the finding published in *Doing Business 2008* that 'Countries that make it easier to pay taxes and contributions also have higher rates of workforce participation, and lower rates of unemployment, among women' (Dennis and Shepherd, 2007). It suggests that this is because a burdensome tax system disproportionately hurts smaller businesses, especially in the services sector, and this is where most women work. This underlines the importance of recognising the implications of tax compliance costs for countries wishing to achieve economic growth.

Background to the Administrative Burdens Reduction Exercise (ABRE)

In 1994, the Dutch started to focus on reducing the administrative burden of regulation. Their approach does not question the policy objectives of the regulations themselves, but seeks to ensure that the way they are implemented imposes the lowest level of costs (see BRTF, 2005: 18).

The Standard Cost Model (SCM) was developed[4] to provide a simplified, consistent method for estimating the administrative costs imposed on business by central government. It aims to provide estimates that are consistent across policy areas by taking a pragmatic approach to measurement, resulting in estimates that are indicative rather than statistically representative.

The approach has three components:

1. Measurement of the burden.
2. Political commitment to a target.
3. An organisational structure that provides incentives to achieve that target.

Details of the international SCM framework can be found in the Administrative Burden Declaration[5] (which summarises the SCM approach) and the International Standard Cost Model Manual.[6]

According to the UK Standard Cost Model Manual (BRE, 2005), a key strength of the SCM is that it is uses a high degree of detail in the measurement of the administrative costs, in

---

4   The SCM was initially developed in the Netherlands and has also been extensively applied in Denmark. A number of other countries have used it to measure the burden of particular regulations.

5   Available at http://www.administrative-burdens.com/publications: *Delivering Reductions in Administrative Burdens*.

6   The International Standard Cost Manual is available at http://www.administrative-burdens.com/publications.

particular going down to the level of individual activities. The result of a measurement is only an estimate, however, and owing to the limited sample size and non-random sample design should not be regarded as necessarily being representative in statistical terms. Even so,

> ... experience in both the Netherlands and Denmark shows that businesses are better able to assess time and resource consumption in connection with the individual regulations using the SCM approach than with methods used previously in both countries. In addition the method's strength is that it is highly action-orientated, which works well as part of a broader regulatory simplification programme. It enables parts of regulations that are particularly difficult for businesses to comply with to be identified. (ibid.: 11)

UK implementation of the Dutch SCM Model

In the 2006 Budget Statement it was announced that HMRC's estimate of the information obligations of taxation amounted to £5.1 billion, based on the Standard Cost Model data collected by KPMG. Despite the weaknesses of the SCM data collection exercise caused by small sample sizes (ibid.), this estimate seems broadly realistic, assuming that large firms incur very small compliance costs as a result of the cash-flow benefits from retaining PAYE and VAT collected on behalf of government until the due date for payment to HMRC.

An analysis of four elements of the KPMG administrative burdens estimates of the burden of taxation has been produced by Sloan (2007), who used the compliance cost outcomes from earlier research by the team at Manchester Business School within the tax model developed for modelling the incidence of direct taxation on the UK SME population[7] (Kauser et al. 2001, 2005; Chittenden, Kauser and Poutziouris, 2005; Chittenden, Poutziouris et al. 2005).

The four outputs from the research that enable estimates of the main tax compliance requirements to be derived from the model are:

- Operating a Pay-As-You-Earn and National Insurance (PAYE/NIC) scheme.
- Complying with Income Tax Self-Assessment for the self-employed.
- Requirement for companies to self-assess their Corporation Tax liability.
- Complying with the VAT system.

For each form of compliance costs, the model uses data for the year 2004/05 to estimate the total compliance costs for the UK SME sector. This enables a comparison to be made between the model estimates for the SME sector and the recent administration burdens project carried out by KPMG on behalf of HMRC.[8] This comparison, however, is not straightforward, and there are a number of difficulties that should be considered when interpreting the outcomes. The first is that the modelling work at Manchester Business School considers only those incorporated firms with up to 250 employees and unincorporated firms with

---

7   For details of the tax modelling work at Manchester Business School, see Sloan (2007) and the earlier developmental work reported by Chittenden et al. (1999b).
8   For further details, see http://www.hmrc.gov.uk/better-regulation/kpmg.htm, last accessed 28 July 2008. Statistics used for comparison are taken from Volume 1, Table 3 on page 20.

up to twenty employees. Second, the KPMG project measured administration burdens rather than full compliance costs, therefore omitting one-off costs, such as learning, when a new regulation or requirement is introduced. Further, the KPMG study used statistically weak samples.[9] Thus, while the KPMG study creates an index for government, the results are not necessarily generalisable or replicable.

Table 18 summarises the outcomes of the KPMG exercise and the aggregated estimates of compliance costs at the level of the SME sector.

Table 18 **Comparison of the KPMG administrative burdens outcomes and compliance costs research**

	MBS modelling estimate (£ billion)	KPMG administrative burdens (£ billion)	Modelling estimate as percentage of KPMG
VAT compliance	£0.662	£1.02	68
PAYE/NIC compliance	£1.626	£0.759	214
Corporation Tax Self-Assessment compliance	£0.803	£0.608	132
Owners' Income Tax Self-Assessment compliance	£0.842	£0.857	98

Source: Extracts from the KPMG ABME report (KPMG LLP, 2006: 27)

In summary, for Corporation Tax Self-Assessment and Income Tax Self-Assessment, the figures obtained in the modelling work at Manchester Business School are reasonably close to those estimated by the KPMG administration burdens exercise; the VAT compliance figures are underestimated in the analysis,

9   See KPMG LLP (2006: Vol. 1, Annex A, p. 36) and presentation on website by Craig Richardson, HMRC, outlining the sampling by the rule of three.

compared with the KPMG data. The PAYE/NIC compliance costs are, prima facie, the least favourable when compared with the KPMG study. The reason for this would appear to be primarily that other elements of payroll activities have been associated with PAYE/NIC in the MBS compliance cost study, and therefore the KPMG figure would provide a more sensible estimate. Excluding this anomaly, therefore, the KPMG figures would appear to be highly credible.

Improvements in information and communications technology

The explosion in electronic means of data handling and communication has resulted in benefits for both taxpayers and HMRC.

In the UK one of the major steps towards reducing the compliance costs on taxpayers has been the combining of HMCE and the Inland Revenue into a single department: HM Revenue and Customs (HMRC). The new HMRC was found to be one of the four government departments which together contribute 75 per cent of the total administrative burdens in the UK (NAO, 2007: 16), as a consequence of which targets and plans have been put in place to achieve simplification and a reduction in the administrative burden.

This newly formed department was given targets (in the 2006 Budget) for reducing the administrative burden by 2010/11, based on the Standard Cost Model (SCM),[10] in the following ways:

---

10 The report on the measurement of the administrative burdens and detail of the Standard Cost Model is available at: www.hmrc.gov.uk/better-regulation/kpmg. htm.

- reducing by at least 10 per cent the administrative burden on business of dealing with HMRC forms and returns, over a five-year period (equivalent to £337 million); and
- reducing the administrative burden on compliant business of dealing with HMRC's audits and inspections by 10 per cent over three years, and at least 15 per cent over five years (equivalent to £14 million and £21 million respectively).

The HMRC 2007 report indicates progress towards achieving these targets, but it must be noted that the department is striving to achieve them against a background of a relatively new merger (2005) and further targets for efficiency gains (the government's 5 per cent per annum efficiency savings programme).

KPMG's research[11] has shown that 85 obligations relating to dealing with forms and returns impose 85 per cent of total administrative compliance costs. As noted above, HMRC aim to reduce the time needed to deal with their forms and returns by at least 10 per cent over five years; and reduce the burden of HMRC's audits and inspections by 10 per cent over three years and at least 15 per cent over five years. These latter targets appear to be based upon the costs of audit and inspection only.[12] A significant proportion of these proposed compliance cost savings will result from online filing and payments, as recommended by the Carter report (below).

---

11 *A Strong and Strengthening Economy: Investing in Britain's Future*, available at http://www.hm-treasury.gov.uk/budget/budget_06/press_notices/bud_budo6_press01.cfm, last accessed 22 September 2008.

12 *Progress towards a New Relationship: How HMRC is working to make life easier for business*, available at http://www.hmrc.gov.uk/budget2006/new-relationship.pdf, last accessed 22 September 2008.

The Carter proposals

The Carter report[13] encouraged HMRC to offer online filing and payment facilities, and in some cases (e.g. PAYE) these will, or have already, become mandatory.

Following publication of this report, HMRC began to invest in online infrastructure and systems leading to the following changes:

- More businesses being required to file e-VAT returns and make electronic payments. Estimated annual savings are £20 per trader – excluding those adopting Annual Accounting or making payments on account.[14]
- A transition to PAYE year-end online filing by May 2010 and the filing of in-year forms (the P45 and P46) from 2010 (estimated saving £3 to £5 per form).
- Corporation Tax returns and accounts (using XBRL[15]) will have to be filed online in phases from April 2010 for all businesses (estimated annual saving to accountants £20 per filing).
- From 2008, filing deadlines for Income Tax Self-Assessment returns were originally set to be 30 September on paper or 30 November online (now changed to 31 October and 31 January respectively for 2008), with the enquiry window linked to the filing date, to encourage early online filing.

---

13 Lord Carter of Coles, *Review of HMRC Online Services*, available at http://www.hmrc.gov.uk/budget2006/carter-review.pdf, last accessed 22 September 2008.

14 *Partial Regulatory Impact Assessment for Increasing Use of Online Services* (RIA), available at http://www.hmrc.gov.uk/ria/pria-online-services.pdf, last accessed 22 September 2008.

15 XBRL stands for eXtensible Business Reporting Language. It is a language for the electronic communication of business and financial data, one of a family of 'XML' languages, which is becoming a standard means of communicating information between businesses and on the Internet.

- From April 2008, computer-generated paper 'substitute' returns for Income Tax Self-Assessment will no longer be accepted (90 per cent of the 3 million substitute returns are filed by agents; online filing was estimated to save between £18 and £25 for simpler returns and up to £90 for the more complex returns).

The expected benefits of these changes are to be found in Table 19.

Table 19 **Expected total benefit to taxpayers from 2012**

	Number of taxpayers affected	Total annual benefit, £m
VAT	2 million	£42
Corporation Tax	1.8 million	£36
PAYE in Year	1.8 million employers filing 20.8 million forms	£62–104
Income Tax Self-Assessment	(Switching from substitute returns to online) – 1.4 million	£25–35
Income Tax Self-Assessment	(Switching from standard returns to online filing – triggered by differential filing dates) – 1 million	£10–30

Source: *Partial Regulatory Impact Assessment for Increasing Use of Online Services*, available at http://www.hmrc.gov.uk/ria/pria-online-services.pdf, last accessed 22 September 2008

In 2005, the estimated total benefits for business were between £158 million and £215 million per annum from 2012/13. Estimated savings to government were expected to increase to £59 million per year by 2014/15.

Further simplifications have been introduced in the UK
Flat Rate VAT Scheme (FRS)

The Flat Rate VAT Scheme is available to businesses with turn-overs of less than £150,000 to facilitate simpler bookkeeping, and as a result lower the costs of compliance. The anticipated savings in costs of compliance as a result of taking up the FRS were estimated by HMCE at an average of £600 per VAT trader per year.[16]

VAT Cash and Annual Accounting Schemes

The VAT Cash and Annual Accounting Schemes (CAS and AAS) are further simplification measures. Thresholds for taxable supplies for joining and leaving the schemes were increased by 10 per cent in 2004, much higher than inflation. The limits became £660,000 for joining and £825,000 for leaving. As a result some businesses were able to stay in the scheme and more firms were able to join. In addition, more businesses would find the CAS scheme attractive with the introduction of bad debt relief and changes to the exit rules intended to reduce compliance costs. The regulatory impact assessment (RIA)[17] estimated the savings in compliance costs to businesses as:

- 6,500 businesses saving £95 per annum in CAS;
- 13,000 businesses saving £75 per annum in the AAS.

---

16 Figure published in *Compliance Cost Review*, http://www.hmrc.gov.uk/ccr/index-archive.htm: VAT schemes, various dates, last accessed 22 September 2008.

17 Available at http://www.hmce.gov.uk/forms/graphics/ria-cash-accounting.pdf.

Total savings to businesses in compliance costs were estimated to be in the order of £1.6 million.[18]

Recent data (HM Treasury, 2007) indicates, however, that only about 1 per cent of those businesses eligible to use the AAS currently do so, with around 95 per cent of all VAT-registered businesses using the current 'default' quarterly returns system.

VAT compliance costs

The MBS Tax Models currently estimate that VAT compliance costs for small firms total £662 million per year (Sloan, 2007), as noted above. This figure compares with the KPMG estimates of the Administrative Burdens of VAT totalling £1 billion for all businesses in the economy. These costs are regressive, i.e. they fall more heavily on small firms than on larger businesses, and so the Chancellor again increased the VAT registration threshold in the 2007 Budget from £61,000 to £64,000. In addition, following changes in EU regulations, the Chancellor doubled the turnover limit for VAT Cash Accounting to £1.35 million, thus allowing an additional 56,500 firms to join the scheme, although if existing experience remains a reasonable guide, only about one third of these businesses will actually do so.

According to the Cash Accounting Regulatory Impact Assessment[19] the main benefit is from interest savings per user of £150. The administrative costs and savings are relatively small, leading to a net ongoing compliance cost saving of £156.60 per business. Given that HMRC finds that about one third of eligible firms join

---

18   Calculated from RIA assessment figures.
19   Available at http://www.hmrc.gov.uk/ria/ria-vat-cas.pdf, accessed 29 September 2008.

the scheme, the compliance cost savings resulting from the extension to the scheme are likely to amount to £3 million,[20] which compares with VAT compliance costs of £694 million (above) in the MBS SBS Tax Models.

Simplifying Income Tax Self-Assessment

The 2005 Budget Statement also reported that Income Tax Self-Assessment (ITSA) compliance costs would be reduced by £5 million per annum by shortening to four pages (a reduction of twelve pages) the tax return forms for 500,000 very small traders. The MBS SBS Tax Models estimate that a saving of £10 per firm from this measure appears realistic and that this would lead to an aggregate compliance cost saving of £5 million, equivalent to 0.2 per cent of total ITSA compliance costs in the MBS SBS Tax Models.

The new Construction Industry Scheme

The long-awaited new Construction Industry Scheme came into force on 6 April 2007. This new legislation is of importance to the small business sector as it affects about one million businesses, most of which are small. The scheme has two objectives. The first is to reduce the administrative burdens of operating the system for taxing subcontractors in the construction sector. The second is to ensure that subcontractors are correctly classified as either employed or self-employed.

---

20 Calculated as follows: 56,500 eligible firms/one third take-up/£156.60 average annual saving = £2.949 million.

In the RIA dated 9 March 2004[21] the scheme was estimated to affect:

- 4,000 large and medium-sized businesses;
- 770,000 sole traders; and
- 200,000 small companies and partnerships.

These numbers are likely to have increased since, however.

The new scheme replaces the existing registration cards, tax certificates and vouchers with a registration process for new subcontractors, and initial verification and monthly confirmation of employment status. According to the RIA the scheme is anticipated to reduce industry compliance costs by £22 million per annum,[22] although there will have been initial set-up costs of between £52 million and £60 million. The initial set-up costs and the ongoing cost of the new scheme are likely to be substantially understated in the RIA as the KPMG Administrative Burdens Collection Exercise shows the costs of the Construction Industry Scheme to be much higher at £321 million.[23] In the short term, however, there will be considerable uncertainty associated with introduction of the new computer system and the impact on the industry of the new employment test.

A note of caution: volume of legislation

Despite UK attempts at reducing the administrative and

---

21   Available at http://www.hmrc.gov.uk/budget2004/cis.pdf, accessed 29 September 2008.

22   RIA, p. 5.

23   KPMG LLP (2006: Table 3, p. 20).

compliance cost burdens noted above, there remains concern in some quarters at the sheer volume of new law introduced in each year's UK Finance Act. The Institute of Chartered Accountants in England and Wales (ICAEW) has been monitoring the trend over the last 30 years and finds that:

> The 2007 Finance Act, at 309 pages, is considerably smaller than the 506 page Finance Act in 2006 and brings the average number of pages in the Finance Acts in the current decade down from 505 to 463 pages. Nevertheless even this lesser figure is more than three times the average size, 153 pages, of Finance Acts at the beginning of the 1980s.[24]

This is significant, as a recent ACCA study (Chittenden and Foster, 2008b) finds overwhelming support across the six countries[25] for the hypothesis that it is the volume of directives, laws and regulations which has the greatest effect on the complexity of tax systems. The large number of pages added to the legislation each year contributes to the complexity of the tax system. This illustrates the daunting task facing the average taxpayer in terms of the cost (psychic and financial) of acquiring and maintaining the knowledge necessary to meet taxation compliance requirements.

---

24 ICAEW's *Big Ben Statutory Tax Burden*, available at http://www.icaew.com/index.cfm/route/150444/icaew_ga/en/Home/Press_ and_policy/Press_releases/ICAE_welcomes_reduction_in_size_of_Finance_ Act, accessed 30 September 2008.

25 A survey of ACCA members with an interest in taxation was carried out in the following countries: Australia, Canada, Hong Kong, Singapore, the USA and the UK.

Concluding remarks

Three major aspects of compliance costs have clearly emerged:

- Compliance costs are high, however measured – in absolute money terms, as a percentage of tax paid, as a percentage of GDP or in comparison to administrative costs.
- Compliance costs are very regressive, especially for VAT/GST (Goods and Services Tax). The level of compliance costs is of particular concern to small business.
- Research into tax compliance costs, and the ensuing publicity, 'puts compliance costs on the political agenda'. Such research has played a significant role in the development by various OECD countries of regulatory impact assessments to evaluate the compliance costs of new tax regulations.

Advanced economies have seen a proliferation of legislation (both tax- and employment-related) in recent decades which, it is argued, has resulted in a mushrooming in the numbers of small firms – which bear the brunt of the regressive compliance costs associated with the resultant legal responsibilities.

As a result, the early part of the 21st century has seen a number of initiatives designed to curb the extent of compliance costs. These have included the World Bank *Doing Business* study, which ranks countries for the ease of paying taxes (among other things), the Administrative Burdens Reduction Exercise and use of the Standard Cost Model, and finally the recent attempts by the UK government to introduce simplifications to tax legislation and filing requirements, which are intended to lead to a reduction in tax compliance costs.

These initiatives, however, are being implemented against a

background of increasing volumes of legislation resulting from attempts to fine-tune the tax system, and to use it to influence behaviour and to shore up the flagging economy. It remains to be seen how successful such programmes may be, given also the drive for efficiency savings within government departments.

As noted in Chapter 1, currently the best estimate of the compliance costs of taxation that fall on business relate to 2005 and amount to £5.1 billion. Indexing this with inflation to 2008 gives a conservative estimate of £5.7 billion, assuming generously that improvements in technology and productivity have offset real increases in salaries and that there has been no net price inflation since then. Adding the OECD estimates of HMRC's administrative costs that were given as £4.8 billion (excluding IT costs) in 2007 again adjusted for inflation gives £5.0 billion. In addition, Boys Smith's estimate that taxpayers subject to self-assessment incur £1.25 billion of costs for tax advice must be included, thus yielding a conservative estimate of the total hidden costs of taxation of £12 billion. This is 2.7 per cent of total tax receipts in 2008/09. As noted in Chapter 1, this is likely to be an underestimate given that, in 1986/87, following a period of simplification of the UK tax system and prior to self-assessment, Sandford estimated that total administrative and compliance costs amounted to 3.75 per cent of tax receipts, equivalent in current terms to £16.75 billion: Sandford's studies were more comprehensive than more recent studies. Given the added complexity and increased numbers of taxes (e.g. Insurance Premium Tax, airport taxes) and different tax rates and allowances, £20 billion would seem more realistic. For the purpose of conservatism, however, the authors suggest that current figures show that the hidden costs of taxation are likely to fall within the range of £12 billion to £17 billion, equivalent to 3p to 4p on the basic rate of Income Tax.

5 FUTURE TRENDS

Introduction

This chapter discusses the implications for the hidden costs of taxation of current trends in tax policy and its implementation. Evans (2003a: 72) expressed hope that increased information arising out of research into the costs of complying with the tax system would continue to be evident in the policymaking process. He emphasises the link between tax law design and implementation, and his view is that 'Sensible tax law design must be informed by an understanding of the impact that design will have on the burden that taxpayers will face and the administrative costs that the revenue authority will be required to carry.' Thus he is clear that the process of tax law design should include an assessment of the impact of the proposed changes on the operating costs of the tax system. He suggests that the greatest contribution that research into tax operating costs can make in the future is to ensure that 'those who formulate and implement legislative change are properly informed as to the operating cost implications of their actions'. He argues that this has been too often ignored in the past and should not continue. It is clear from this chapter that this message has not been heeded.

Pope ((1992), quoted in ibid.: 73), however, describes an evolution in the stages of awareness of compliance costs, ranging from initial neglect, then recognition by practitioners, quantification (generally by academics), policy recognition, effective policy measures resulting in lower compliance costs and finally continual monitoring of compliance costs. As such it is to be hoped that we are still in the midst of the process that will lead to compliance costs being fully taken into account by policymakers.

Complexity of legislation

The prime causes of high compliance costs are identified by Evans (2003b) as the complexity of legislative provisions combined with the frequency of legislative change. This shows no sign of abating, particularly in the UK, where despite frequent promises of simplification by successive Chancellors, 'It is generally reckoned that the UK has the longest tax code in the world, having recently overtaken India'[1] (Truman, 2008).

The content of the Chartered Institute of Taxation (CIOT) exams indicates the increase in complexity as well as the additional volume of tax legislation each year. The content of the exams seems almost unrecognisable when compared with that of a few years ago.

Truman (ibid.) argues in favour of addressing the underlying stresses that cause the 'faultlines' in the tax system, rather than continuing to generate a huge volume of legislation to 'paper over the cracks'. He cites the example of Capital Gains Tax (CGT) changes announced in the 2007 pre-Budget report (PBR), which were intended to simplify the system and charge relevant gains at a lower rate of 18 per cent. The outcry from certain sections

---

1   See Annexe to this chapter for the position at July 2006.

of the business community and subsequent vacillation by the Chancellor have resulted in a situation where the ensuing legislation is regarded as opaque by those who are most familiar with it: 'the underlying legislation was botched together like Frankenstein's monster out of odd bits that don't appear to go together' (Thexton, 2008). This uncertainty is bound to increase both the financial and psychic costs of compliance for taxpayers and tax advisers alike, and consequently the administrative costs as HMRC attempt to police it.

Hasseldine (2001: 11) argues that there is a link between compliance and complexity, suggesting that 'a significant part of the problem of tax non-compliance may be attributed to the complexities of tax laws and high compliance costs'. He makes the case for using behavioural research methods to investigate these linkages in order to understand the structural aspects of the tax system which increase the costs to taxpayers of complying with the tax system and thus may contribute to non-compliance.

Income shifting and the Arctic Systems case

An example of where HMRC itself has contributed to both complexity and uncertainty is the (2007) case of *Jones* v. *Garnett (Arctic Systems)*. HMRC pursued the case all the way through the English legal process over a number of years, resulting in a great deal of uncertainty in the area of SME tax planning during that time. The legislation was apparently unclear to both the tax officials and tax advisers and, even though the House of Lords has now found in the taxpayer's favour, there remains huge uncertainty because HMRC announced that they would change the law as a result. Discussions continue as to whether a change in the law would be fair, given that the whole basis of the case was that taxpayers legitimately arranged their affairs by choosing, out of two perfectly legal options, the one that would result in a lower tax bill.

The case revolved around the legality of husband and wife shifting income between themselves to minimise their tax bill. Truman (2008) points out, however, that this problem arises because of wider problems in the tax system. It is an example of where complexity has bred complexity and where an inappropriate set of principles for taxation has led to the problem. Truman's view is that where income shifting occurs in 'husband and wife companies' it is merely a response to 'our inflexible system of independent taxation'; and that there is an inconsistency in a system that assesses a couple as two independent taxpayers for Income Tax purposes when they can now transfer Inheritance Tax (IHT) nil-rate bands on death and their joint incomes must be taken into account for tax credit claims.

A related topic is the issue of personal services businesses, and whether it is logical for such a business operated through a company to be treated any differently for tax purposes than the same business operated as a sole trader. Much effort has been expended in maintaining the dividing line between employment and self-employment through the IR35 and managed service company legislation.[2] In the modern world, however, Truman (ibid.) argues, the economic reality is that there is a spectrum of activity between full employment and the running of an entrepreneurial business, ranging through temporary contract work,

---

2   See also *Dragonfly Consultancy Limited* v. *HMRC* (2008), http://www.bailii.org/cgi-bin/markup.cgi?doc=/ew/cases/EWHC/Ch/2008/2113.html&query=dragonfly&method=boolean, accessed 17 October 2008.

a portfolio of part-time appointments and freelancing; and in practice there is often very little difference between these from the point of view of the person doing the work and the person hiring them to do it.

Global comparisons of tax systems promote transparency

Pressure from global studies and from intellectual work in the business sector still prevails and, because of the international comparisons this leads to, may be fruitful in the long run. As discussed in a previous chapter, the World Bank *Doing Business* series provides useful trends over time of the ease of doing business. Included within its report are measurements of the ease of paying taxes. The UK ranked 12th for the ease of paying taxes in 2008, but in the 2009 report had slipped to 16th, while retaining the rank of 6th for the overall ease of doing business.[3] The *Doing Business 2009* overview (p. 7) notes that simplifying regulation helps business and government alike. Typically businesses will save time and the government saves money as a result of reduced administration costs.

PwC collaborated with the World Bank in this study and their report is published as *Paying Taxes: The Global Picture* (2007). They find that burdensome tax systems can be a deterrent and can lead to tax evasion. Companies in 90 per cent of the countries surveyed ranked tax administration among the top five obstacles to doing business. The main factors cited as contributing to this are:

---

3   Early indications from *Doing Business 2010* are that the UK has remained at 16th for the ease of paying taxes, but has moved up to 5th for the ease of doing business.

- The large number of taxes business must pay.
- Lengthy and complex tax administration.
- Complex tax legislation.
- High tax rates.

PwC argue that to help with paying taxes and implementing reform, governments should consider all aspects of a tax system. The total tax contribution should be recognised, i.e. all taxes borne and collected together with the related compliance costs. There appear, however, to be mixed views about the influence of business over the regulatory regime. At a recent conference a majority of (mainly civil service) attendees believed that 'The regulatory regime favours business over consumers' interests' (LBRO, 2008).

Arguing in favour of simplification of tax law, PwC (2007: 21) state:

> The boldest reform is to simplify tax law so that every business faces the same tax burden – with no exemptions, tax holidays or special treatment for large or foreign businesses. Many tax laws start that way. But when hard times come and governments need revenue, tax rates are often raised. This is unpopular, and large or well-connected businesses usually obtain special treatment. Soon the tax law becomes riddled with exceptions, generally at the expense of small businesses, which have the least ability to lobby. Often they are pushed into the informal sector.

PwC are keen to promote the message that there are benefits to business and to government from tax reform. Evidence from the survey shows that tax reform creates more vibrant businesses and a smaller tax burden encourages firms to invest.

Furthermore, streamlining taxes increases the positive effect, leading to increased productivity.[4] From the government point of view, a complicated tax system costs a lot of money to run; therefore streamlining it will release funds that could be better spent on education, healthcare and infrastructure. 'Tax reforms inspire political debate and can be hotly contested. But both businesses and government benefit when taxes are simple and fair and set incentives for growth' (ibid.: 15).

Trends in taxation systems

Indirect taxes

PwC (ibid.: 25) report that the actual trends in taxation show that there is a general and increasing shift from direct taxation to indirect taxation (consumption taxes). They suggest that many governments expect their major source of revenue in the future to be from VAT/GST, and that this transition requires careful planning to ensure that the system introduced delivers optimum levels of tax revenue with the least possible adverse impact on individuals and businesses. PwC argue that a joint approach between government and business is required for a successful outcome, because with VAT/GST businesses are the 'unpaid' tax collectors. Indirect taxes are popular with governments because they are generally regarded as a less visible form of taxation.

Consumption taxes are also seen as vital in demonstrating a tax structure that is conducive to growth and employment while maintaining tax revenues. Tax competition between countries has resulted in lowering direct taxes on income (including corporate

---

4   A study in India estimates that tax reform can increase productivity by up to 60 per cent (PwC, 2007: 14).

Income Tax and Capital Gains Tax); in order to maintain revenue levels, consumption taxes have increased in response.

Consumption taxes may cause new compliance costs for businesses in terms of labour and IT costs for producing documentation, and also the associated reporting and filing of returns. PwC argue that a pure VAT/GST should not generate any impact in the profit and loss account of a business, nor should it result in any double taxation. Also it should not generate disproportionate compliance costs or risks which require the input of costly management time when collecting the taxes on behalf of government. They note, however, that recent studies have shown (e.g. Chittenden, Poutziouris et al., 2005) that the compliance cost burden varies considerably between large and small businesses, therefore challenging the view that VAT is a neutral tax. PwC (2007: 27) suggest that the reasons for this are the lack of common global VAT/GST principles and the increasing complexity of the legislation, combined with lack of guidance from the tax authorities, all of which leads to uncertainty, which in turn increases compliance costs and risks. The problem of international VAT fraud has now reached such proportions that economy and finance ministers of the EU member states have settled on a general approach to strengthen the fight against it (Faith, 2008). The proposals will focus in particular on VAT carousels – fraud circuits which target cross-border transactions. The article (in *International Tax Review*, 11 November 2008) quotes a UK-based tax adviser: 'VAT fraud is a very big problem. The tax accounts for 20% of turnover on average in Europe so it significantly affects profit margins. The UK government estimates that it loses billions of pounds to VAT fraud.' Any response could well make compliance more expensive.

On the other hand, both PwC (ibid.: 27) and the OECD (2006) recommend that legal certainty be achieved regarding VAT/GST by the adoption of internationally accepted principles, thereby reducing compliance costs. PwC (ibid.) note that tax authorities are attempting to simplify compliance through the better use of technology. As the number of taxpayers making use of these facilities increases, the tax authorities recoup their initial investment through improved administration efficiencies.

Use of technology

The position with regard to small firms and the use of technology is reported by the Small Enterprise Research Team in Quarter 2 of 2007 (SERT, 2007). A key finding from this report was that, at the time, government regulations and paperwork remained the biggest single problem facing small business. The report also indicated continued increases in the number of firms adopting new technologies – although, as we have seen in earlier chapters, the use of electronic media for tax compliance does not generally lead to a reduction in the cost of tax compliance (KPMG LLP, 2006).

There is a danger, too, that governments will believe that new technology reduces the cost of tax administration to businesses significantly and will respond by increasing the number of taxes that businesses will be required to remit or collect.

A further use for technology by HMRC is discussed by Shaw et al. (2008: 48). They report the trend over the last couple of decades for Nordic countries to send out tax return forms that have been pre-completed with information already held by the tax authority. Taxpayers then merely check the pre-completed information and complete the areas that are blank. They note that pre-completion has a number of advantages (OECD, 2007) in that it offers the potential for significant savings in taxpayer compliance costs because taxpayers will have to spend less time completing their returns. Also, because taxpayer errors are avoided in pre-completed sections, this will reduce the administrative resources required to deal with incorrect returns. Shaw et al. (2008) point out, however, that individuals may be less likely to report income missed by a pre-completed return. Additionally, they suggest that pre-completion is very demanding from the tax authority's point of view, as the information held needs to be accurate and the tax authority must be able to link together all information relating to a given taxpayer soon after the end of the tax year. They state that, historically, HMRC have not found this straightforward, although as part of the next section, we report areas where HMRC are currently considering pre-completion.

HMRC progress with administrative burdens

HMRC are required to provide an annual update on their progress with simplification and reducing the administrative burden. In 2008 this was published in the following two documents accompanying the 2008 Budget:

- *The Framework for a Better Relationship: Making a difference: review of links with large business.*
- *Delivering a New Relationship with Business: Progress on HMRC's plans to improve the SME customer experience.*

Discussions with business have stressed the importance of a fair, equitable and competitive tax system which provides certainty, stability and predictability (HMRC, 2008b). HMRC also recognise SMEs as a significant business customer group, being responsible for the collection of around 40 per cent of all HMRC taxes in 2006 (HMRC, 2008a: 3) and upon whom 88 per cent of the business tax administrative burden falls. A stated objective of HMRC is not only to achieve numerical targets, but also to make a noticeable difference to businesses' experience of the tax system. In the 2007 Budget it was announced that HMRC had delivered combined administrative burdens savings of £170 million towards the targets that require: i) reduction in dealing with forms and returns of £337 million over five years and ii) reduction in audits and inspections of £35 million over five years. The 2008 papers explain how HMRC has met its administrative burden challenge over the previous twelve months. They estimate that the switch to easier online filing and payment will reduce the administrative burden by £15–20 million during the target period (to 2012). The main tax return had been redesigned and was in place for 2007/08, and from April 2008 certain boxes were to be pre-completed with data from HMRC's other systems (e.g. under-payments brought forward, state pension and student loan indicators), reducing the circumstances in which taxpayers have to provide the same information more than once.

The proposed European Union (EU) changes to reduce Intrastat coverage will remove 13,500 UK businesses from the obligation to complete Intrastat forms, and it is anticipated that this change will reduce administrative burdens by £3.5 million per annum (ibid.: 9). Further changes to reduce the administrative burden of forms and returns specifically benefiting employers and the self-employed are expected to save £56 million towards the target. With regard to audit and inspection, HMRC will use a differentiated approach towards taxpayers displaying different types of behaviour (compliant or otherwise); this will be achieved by a risk-based approach and a range of targeted interventions to be carried out quickly and efficiently. It is estimated that the simplification of other areas, e.g. the capital allowances system, the Construction Industry Scheme and VAT reforms, will reduce administrative burdens by £15 million per annum, and a simplification of Stamp Duty relating to UK registered shares and securities is expected to deliver savings of almost £14 million per annum.

Additional support (which requires new resources within the department) will also be made available to assist taxpayers in understanding their obligations and complying with the tax system. As noted previously, however, HMRC may struggle to provide this support at a time when they are also required to achieve efficiency savings.

Other impositions on employers related to the tax system

Ambler et al. (2005: 5) argue that the UK Impact Assessment system does not work to reduce the administrative burden as originally claimed; rather it has facilitated the rapid increase in the burden on business. They use an overall impact assessment scorecard (p. 19) to demonstrate that, on a recurrent basis, businesses are worse off, while government and the consumers receive ongoing net benefits. They suggest this represents a consistent transfer of financial responsibility for government policies that benefit the Exchequer and the individual taxpayer at the expense of business, and that this amounts to an implicit form of business taxation.

Other areas where government imposes obligations on

employers which are not dissimilar to the obligations they already .
bear in terms of collecting taxes were summarised in a recent
Treasury Committee report:

> Today an employer is potentially responsible for: three
> types of NI (Class 1, 1a and 1b); payment of tax credits;
> collection of Student Loans; four statutory payments
> (Statutory Sick Pay, Statutory Paternity Pay, Statutory
> Adoption Pay, Statutory Maternity Pay); the Construction
> Industry Scheme tax; [and] monitoring National Minimum
> Wage compliance. These are of course only the obligations
> administered by the Inland Revenue. (House of Commons
> Treasury Committee, 2004: 10)

Also employers are required to administer assorted savings
schemes, share save schemes and payroll payment. Since the
report was published we understand that, of these, payment of
tax credits is no longer imposed on employers. Nevertheless, there
are significant obligations imposed on employers that are related
to the tax and benefits system which do not directly involve
collecting taxes.

Indeed, these obligations are shortly to increase. The Department for Work and Pensions (DWP) proposes the introduction of
personal pension savings accounts ('personal accounts') in 2012.
This issue is particularly topical and of concern to small businesses as it has been acknowledged by Lord Turner[5] himself that

---

5   Lord Turner was the author of a Pensions Commission report in 2005 that out-
    lined the need for reform of pensions provision in the UK (Pensions Commis-
    sion, *A New Pensions Settlement for the Twenty-first Century: The Second Report of the
    Pensions Commission*, 2005, available at http://www.webarchive.org.uk/ukwa/
    target/145583, last accessed January 2010). It was upon the findings of this report
    that the DWP based a number of changes to pensions in the UK, one of which is
    the introduction of personal accounts.

'This will be a bigger cost for small business than a big business',[6] and the Forum of Private Business in a recent survey estimated that '72% of respondents could not afford employer compulsory pensions'.[7] Employers will not only have to make contributions to the personal accounts, they will also have to administer the payroll deductions.

Concluding remarks

Thus, there has been recognition by governments worldwide of the need to reduce administrative burdens, including those of the tax system. This has now become and seems set to remain an important part of the political agenda. The OECD has commented: 'The level of attention being given by member countries to administrative burden reduction is currently on a scale not previously witnessed' (OECD, 2008: 45). In this regard, the World Bank *Doing Business* series continues to monitor the ease of paying taxes.

In the UK, HMRC are required to publish their progress with regard to the simplification agenda and the targets for compliance costs reduction; the National Audit Office also report on this. The task for HMRC is doubly challenging as the targets must be achieved at a time when they are also required to make efficiency savings within their own budgets. Furthermore, the current round of the reductions exercise is set to end in 2010, shortly before the intended start of the DWP-proposed personal accounts, which some argue will result in a significant increase in the burden for business.

---

6   BBC, 'Turner defends pension age reform', available at http://news.bbc.co.uk/1/hi/business/4488968.stm, accessed 27 November 2008.

7   FPB, 'Because of you ... ', FPB Annual Report 2006, Knutsford, Cheshire, p. 15.

There is a general acceptance among researchers and practitioners that it is the volume of tax legislation which contributes most to complexity and thus increases compliance costs. The frequency of changes in tax legislation is also important as compliance costs (both financial and psychic) are higher when dealing with a piece of legislation for the first time. Shaw et al. (2008) argue that 'Taxes should therefore be kept as simple and stable as possible', but there is little sign of this objective being achieved. As discussed previously, the costs of compliance are highly regressive and are therefore of increasing importance in the current climate given the growing numbers of small firms.

As the compliance costs of direct taxes are reducing, there appears to be a trend towards indirect taxes, which are regarded as less visible to taxpayers. They are growing as a major source of tax revenue for governments worldwide. PwC (2007: 27) warn that care should be taken in designing VAT/GST systems because of the regressive nature of the associated compliance costs, and the increased complexity arising out of the lack of common global VAT/GST principles. There is a temptation for governments to introduce additional complexity through a proliferation of indirect taxes, thus cancelling out the reduction in administrative burdens achieved with respect to direct taxes.

Annexe

A recent study by PwC looked at the burden of federal (national government) tax administration for the top 20 countries ranked by gross domestic product (GDP). The relative tax administration burden in each country was measured by the number of pages of primary federal tax legislation, as shown in Table 20.

Table 20 **Federal tax administration burden**

Country	GDP ranking	GDP $m	Number of pages of primary tax legislation (ranking)
United States	1	11,711,834	5,100 (5)
Japan	2	4,622,771	7,200 (4)
Germany	3	2,740,551	1,700 (10)
United Kingdom	4	2,124,385	8,300 (2)
France	5	2,046,646	1,300 (13)
China and Hong Kong	6	1,931,710	2,000 (9)
Italy	7	1,677,834	3,500 (7)
Spain	8	1,039,927	530 (17)
Canada	9	977,968	2,440 (8)
India	10	691,163	9,000 (1)
Korea	11	679,674	4,760 (6)
Mexico	12	676,497	1,600 (12)
Australia	13	637,327	7,750 (3)
Brazil	14	603,973	500 (18)
Russia	15	581,447	700 (=15)
Netherlands	16	578,979	1,640 (11)
Switzerland	17	357,542	300 (20)
Belgium	18	352,312	830 (14)
Sweden	19	346,412	700 (=15)
Turkey	20	302,786	350 (19)

Source: PwC study, June/July 2006. GDP information is based on 2004 figures taken from World Bank data as at April 2006. For more information visit: http://www.worldbank.org

It is notable that the second-greatest amount (by volume) of primary tax legislation is in the UK – beaten only by India, which is hardly comparable. The study does not measure state and local taxes. Countries levy taxes at different political levels, which will affect the relative ranking. It is also worth noting, however, that the local taxation system in the UK is relatively inconsequential compared with that of many of the other countries noted above.

6 ISSUES FOR POLICYMAKERS

Introduction

We have seen that the hidden costs of taxation are important and that they comprise administrative costs (tax authority costs) and compliance costs (borne by the taxpayer). An important difference between the two is that there are no distributional effects associated with administrative costs because they are paid for by tax revenue and thus borne by the whole population. This is not the case, however, with compliance costs.

The important factor about compliance costs, as consistently indicated by the research, is their highly regressive nature, as they fall disproportionately on small firms:

> It follows that where small firms are competing in the same market with large firms (as in most retailing for example) they are being put under a state-created competitive disadvantage. They cannot pass on their compliance costs to the same extent as larger firms (whose net compliance costs may, indeed, be nil or negative). They have to take a cut in their rate of profit, or, in the case of small proprietors, perhaps in their leisure. Compliance costs then become a factor helping to push small firms out of particular markets. (Sandford et al., 1989: 200)

Although, as Shaw et al. (2008: 21) noted, ultimate incidence depends on the extent to which prices and wages adjust to shift the burden away from the remitter.

In this chapter we examine those factors which tend to increase the hidden costs of taxation and make suggestions as to the steps government may take to reduce them. It has become apparent during the course of this study that complexity of tax legislation is a key factor in increasing the hidden costs of taxation: 'Complexity and lack of clarity in tax law in general will make for higher administrative and compliance costs' (ibid.: 20). Furthermore, we have reached the view that it will not be possible to substantially reduce compliance costs and the distortions they create by tinkering with the current tax system, but that a more fundamental rethink of tax structures is required. Therefore we examine proposals for simplification of the tax system in general and tax legislation in particular.

Government policy objectives

Sandford et al. (1989: 209) set out four criteria for governments. They should:

(i) Explicitly recognise the importance of compliance costs.
(ii) Resist the temptation to reduce their own administrative costs at the expense of compliance costs.
(iii) Seek to minimise compliance costs, especially for small businesses.
(iv) Be prepared to compensate for compliance costs.

A number of writers have noted the potential conflict between the efficiency objectives being pursued by HMRC and the objective of minimising compliance costs (ibid.: 211), and almost twenty years later the same point was made in the Mirrlees Review.

To reduce both administrative and compliance costs attention needs to be paid to the design of the tax system and to tax rates. As Shaw et al. (2008: 3) put it: 'Administrative and compliance costs depend on a wide range of factors, including the complexity of the tax, characteristics of the tax base, structure of tax rates, frequency of reform, and organisation and efficiency of the tax authority.' Shaw et al. argue in favour of keeping taxes as simple and stable as possible. They also note that in some areas there is a trade-off between administrative and compliance costs, depending on where the responsibility for calculating the tax liability falls, i.e. on the tax authority or the taxpayer. Thus, if the tax authority provides help and guidance to taxpayers, this increases administration costs but reduces compliance costs.

Key issues for reducing administrative and compliance costs are identified by Shaw et al. (ibid.: 20):

- The use of common definitions and procedures across taxes reduces costs by decreasing the number of calculations that have to be made, e.g. for Income Tax and National Insurance.
- Characteristics of the tax base: physical size and mobility; whether there is compulsory registration.
- Structure of tax rates: simplified schemes can be counterproductive because taxpayers calculate their liability against all possible schemes and choose the lowest (therefore increasing compliance costs).
- The cost of understanding: which tax-related obligations apply to the taxpayer and what needs to be done to comply

with them; 'stability is a highly desirable feature of a tax system, since learning what to do is much more costly the first time than on subsequent occasions'.

Sandford et al. (1989: 212) discuss the minimisation of compliance costs under the following broad headings: temporary compliance costs; regular compliance costs; relations between taxes; and borderlines between taxes. These broad headings are a useful way of thinking about the problem today.

Temporary compliance costs

Temporary compliance costs are described as 'once and for all' start-up costs and also learning costs. To minimise these costs, stability should be an essential feature of the tax system.

An important factor in achieving stability is for the government to get legislation right the first time, which requires an effective process of consultation before passing and enacting tax legislation. Recent examples of where the process has been found to be wanting are:

- *The 0 per cent starting rate of Corporation Tax:* This was originally introduced in 2002 to allow small limited companies to pay no Corporation Tax on profits of up to £10,000. As a result, thousands of sole traders and partnerships became incorporated to take advantage of the relief, only for the rules to be changed three years later as an anti-avoidance measure.
- *The 10 per cent starting rate of Income Tax 'simplification' fiasco:* The 10 per cent tax rate was introduced in 1999 by Gordon

Brown for income up to the first £1,500 over the personal allowance. It was abolished in 2008/09, and the manner of its disappearance caused some anger as it was announced almost as a footnote in Gordon Brown's final Budget in 2007, although the full implications of the move were apparently not appreciated by most people until Alistair Darling's first Budget in March 2008. The government claimed this was a move towards simplification; this is not entirely true, however, as the 10 per cent rate still applies to some savings income and changes were made to the benefits system to compensate many losers. It can be argued that the 10 per cent rate should never have been introduced or that it should never have been scrapped. But the way in which the policy was brought in, partially reversed and then compensation offered to those suffering from the reversal imposed costs.

- *The reduction of 2.5 per cent in the standard rate of VAT at the start of the Christmas season in 2008:* It is difficult to imagine a more inconvenient time to change the VAT rate. Experts estimated the cost of the reduction as £500 per registered company or £850 million in total.[1] Figures from Derek Allen of the Institute of Chartered Accountants in Scotland (ICAS) suggest that the cost of reinstating the cut will be even higher, approaching £1 billion,[2] calling into question the Treasury's much lower estimates.

Compliance costs may also be minimised by keeping the

1 http://www.accountancyage.com/accountancyage/news/2242226/vat-figure-gross-underestimate, accessed 10 June 2009.
2 http://www.accountancyage.com/accountancyage/analysis/2242624/overview-derek-allen-vat-going, accessed 10 June 2009.

frequency of tax changes to a minimum (ibid.: 213) and by ensuring that the timing of changes is convenient to taxpayers, e.g. taking effect from the start of a month, and allowing time for them to make the necessary changes.

Regular compliance costs

Regular compliance costs are those arising out of the tax structure. Sandford et al. (ibid.: 213) note these may be minimised by keeping a tax as simple as possible, e.g. a single rate, minimum borderlines, high threshold, convenient form of threshold, minimum of special exemptions, reliefs and provisions.

Again, taxpayer compliance costs may be kept to a minimum if the tax authorities incur the administrative costs of providing free, easily understood tax information and advice both in printed and electronic forms and verbally.

The tax form is another area where compliance costs may be significantly reduced by designing it to be as short, simple and clear as possible. There have been recent attempts by HMRC to simplify the Self-Assessment return which have had a mixed reception from tax professionals.

Bearing in mind Adam Smith's canon of 'convenience', the method and timing of returns and payments should be convenient to the taxpayer, e.g. tying in with the period of business accounts (ibid.: 214).

Another canon, 'certainty', is also important, because uncertainty increases compliance costs, both financial – owing to the need to seek advice – and psychic – owing to the worry factor of being unsure whether one has complied or not. Sandford et al. (ibid.: 214) found that this was a particular issue with regard to gifts with reservation under the IHT legislation. They make the suggestion that uncertainty may be a product of obscure legislation. Currently, as far as business taxes are concerned, uncertainty continues over the treatment of husband and wife companies following the (2007) case of *Jones* v. *Garnett* (see previous chapter). It seems reasonable to suggest that the tax implications of a transaction should be capable of being understood before the transaction is undertaken (Lymer and Oats, 2008: 49)

Relationships between taxes

Relationships between taxes should also be structured to minimise compliance costs. Sandford et al. (1989: 215) give a general rule that the more taxes there are, the higher compliance costs are likely to be. They suggest that minimising compliance costs is likely to be achieved by 'fewer taxes with broad bases which minimise exemptions and reliefs [and] … fewer taxes at higher rates [rather] than many taxes at lower rates'.

Graetz (2005) argues that in order to create a fair and balanced modern tax system, an ideal and simple solution would comprise a consumption tax combined with an income tax paid by the top 5 per cent of the wealthiest citizens. A fundamental part of this idea is that by removing large numbers of the lower-paid from the direct tax system, the government would save significant administrative costs while potentially maintaining revenues.

Lloyd George (Lymer and Oats, 2008: 15) believed that the tax system should ensure that everyone contributes something to tax revenues, no matter how poor they are. This seems equitable given that public expenditure provides benefits for the common good, but such a policy comes with a cost in terms of administration (in the case of direct taxes) as revenue authorities would need to maintain records for virtually every citizen, regardless of the extent of their capacity to contribute to the public purse. Furthermore, governments might end up paying welfare benefits to those who paid taxes – as happens in the UK.

A reduction in compliance costs may also be achieved by using a common tax base, common definitions and common procedures for taxes. This has been a particular issue with regard to PAYE and National Insurance, which has resulted in calls for the two to be aligned to a common base.

Borderlines between taxes

The borderlines between taxes add to compliance costs as well as causing economic distortion by encouraging taxpayers to try to pay one tax rather than another in respect of a particular economic activity. Sandford et al. (1989: 216) suggest that, where taxpayer behaviour is influenced in this way, it is frequently accompanied by an increase in compliance costs. The conclusion is therefore that tax systems should strive to be neutral. The issue is summarised as follows:

> … [C]ompliance costs are affected by every aspect of
> tax policy, whether it be the introduction of a new tax;
> or a change in the tax structure (such as a reduction in
> the number of rates of VAT or a widening of the income
> tax base); or an alteration in the balance of taxation (for
> example by raising indirect taxes to pay for an increase
> in the income tax threshold); or changes in the method
> of administration (like moving from revenue- to self-
> assessment …). What is important is that the significance
> of compliance costs should be fully recognised and that they

should be consistently taken into account and given due weight in tax policy-making. (Ibid.: 220)

Compensation

Currently it may be argued that there is no real motivation for government or the tax authorities to reduce administrative and compliance costs. Where they are required to reduce administrative costs in order to meet public sector efficiency targets, there may even be a temptation to pass these costs on to the taxpayer in the form of increased compliance costs. One way to focus the minds of government and the tax authorities on this issue would be through the introduction of compensation, as suggested by Sandford et al. (ibid.: 216). Possible options are:

- Differential payment periods for businesses of different sizes, both for VAT and PAYE, to redistribute the cash-flow benefit more equitably between large and small firms.
- Compensation systems for innocent taxpayers incurring costs as a result of an in-depth investigation.
- Where the government specifically transfers a function from the public to the private sector because the private sector can carry it out more efficiently, this will result in a reduction in total operating costs. In this case the government could fully compensate the private sector, at least for the substantial temporary costs incurred, and still be left with a saving.

Complexity of the legislative process

There have been many calls in the last decade to make the UK tax system simpler: two of the Consultative Committees of Accountancy Bodies (CCAB) have made representations to government and the accountancy professions[3] (see Annexe to this chapter); the Chartered Institute of Taxation (CIOT)[4] has produced a number of papers which deal with proposals to simplify specific areas. Additionally, the Smith Institute has recently published a collection of essays in which there are calls for a reduction in complexity.[5] Others suggest that by tolerating this level of complexity, Britain is becoming increasingly disadvantaged in the global business arena: 'To be economically competitive, Britain needs to reduce the burden of tax complexity on businesses and individuals' (Boys Smith et al., 2008: 4).

A sobering parallel in history may be drawn: '… the fall of Rome was fundamentally due to economic deterioration resulting from excessive taxation, inflation, and over-regulation. Higher and higher taxes failed to raise additional revenues because wealthier taxpayers could evade such taxes while the middle class – and its taxpaying capacity – were exterminated' (Bartlett, 1994).

We have discussed, in a previous chapter, the issue of the volume of legislation, but here we examine potential reasons for complexity which appear to be enshrined in the UK process of enacting tax legislation. The causes of complexity in this area have been summarised by Truman (2007, quoting Broke, 1999) as: diversity of aim, volume of legislation, drafting and language.

Truman (ibid.: 3), in examining the progress made by the tax

---

3   http://www.accaglobal.com/pubs/publicinterest/pressandpolicy/unit/manifestos/m4tax_manifesto.pdf.

4   http://www.tax.org.uk.

5   E.g. Chittenden and Foster (2008a).

law rewrite project, likens the UK tax legislation to an outmoded piece of machinery:

> It's as if the tax system were a massive piece of Victorian machinery. Prior to the rewrite, it was rusty and ill-maintained, with corroded pipes held together by gaffer tape. The machinery had been changed and tinkered with over time, so that there were large additional items of plant lashed rather insecurely into the main framework, supported only by a couple of bolts and a frayed rope to take the strain. The room had been expanded over the years to take this extra machinery, and at ceiling level it looked suspiciously as if a load-bearing wall or two had been taken away. Here and there you could see magnificent examples of Victorian ornamentation that served no modern purpose, and the whole construction clanked and heaved and made a tremendous noise whenever you tried to get it to do anything.

He recognises the huge improvements made in terms of the language used, the ordering and layout of sections, and the logical framework in which they are presented, but notes that this merely serves to illustrate how much more needs to be done.

> The problem is that, now we can see clearly what the machinery is doing, the realisation dawns with awful clarity, that much of WHAT it is doing is ridiculously complicated. Pulleys connect with levers and gears, which connect with pistons and pipes and switches; and a tremendous amount of energy is consumed to very little practical effect.

With regard to achieving simplification, Truman's view is that the tax law rewrite project (TLRP) is a start, but he is clear that it is the precursor to a much larger-scale, genuine simplification of the system.

A significant drawback to the TLRP is that '... it was not agreed in 1995 that all new Finance Bill provisions would be written in the new tax law rewrite style. This means that new provisions still written in old style have continued to be added to the existing mountain of legislation, even, in some cases, where the existing legislation was already rewritten by the Project' (House of Commons Treasury Committee, 2004: Ev 99).

Which gives an additional perspective to Howe (2000: 10), speaking of his experience on the TLRP in the face of annual Finance Acts which are longer than results from the TLRP. 'It is like trying to repaint Brighton Pier at a time when its owners are trying to extend it to the French coast.'

We believe it is fundamental to progress in this area that all forthcoming legislation should be constructed in the tax law rewrite style.

Diversity of aim

Traditional views have held that the fundamental aim of taxes is to meet state expenditure. Truman agrees with this insofar as it relates to direct taxes, which he believes should have only one aim: 'to tax each pound received as consistently as possible'. He questions the validity of this assumption with regard to indirect taxes, however, some of which are intended to influence behaviour.

Truman quotes Lord Howe's view that one of the major causes of excessively complex tax legislation is the effect of 'inspirational input from Chancellors who retain the misguided and conceited belief that tax changes can dramatically transform human behaviour'. He criticises attempts to use tax legislation to deliberately distort the market, which more often than not succeed only in creating massive avoidance loopholes without achieving the intended purpose. Truman also believes that the taxation of employee reward packages should be simplified to 'collect the same amount of tax from a reward package regardless of how it was constituted'. He suggests that with this kind of simplification 300 sections of the Income Tax (Earnings and Pensions) Act 2003 (ITEPA, 2003) could be replaced by five.

Volume of legislation and anti-avoidance

Truman (2007) expresses the view, which he believes is widely held, that 'anti-avoidance is the main driver of legislative volume'. He suggests that blocking anti-avoidance schemes individually is likely to be ineffective because this merely creates further loopholes and continues the spiral of increasing legislation. He offers a number of alternatives to suppress tax avoidance: enactment of the *Furniss* v. *Dawson* Principle;[6] purposive drafting (the inclusion of an overall purpose clause at the start of a charging section); and targeted anti-avoidance principles applying to those areas of legislation most prone to avoidance (rather than broad anti-avoidance provisions which are generally considered to increase uncertainty).

---

6   The limits of the principle were summarised by Lord Brightman in *Furness* v. *Dawson* [1984] A.C. 474. In his leading speech Lord Brightman said (at p. 527D–E): '… First, there must be a pre-ordained series of transactions, or, if one likes, one single composite transaction. This composite transaction may or may not include the achievement of a legitimate commercial (i.e. business) end … Secondly, there must be steps inserted which have no commercial (business) *purpose* apart from the avoidance of a liability to tax – not "no business *effect*". If those two ingredients exist, the inserted steps are to be disregarded for fiscal purposes. The court must then look at the end result. Precisely how the end result will be taxed will depend on the terms of the taxing statute sought to be applied.'

Concluding remarks

Complexity in tax legislation occurs as a result of weak policy and processes. More coherent policy would lead to fewer tax rates, fewer tax borderlines and fewer reliefs, leading to lower administrative and compliance costs. Boys Smith et al. (2008: 17) summarise six drivers of this weak policy and processes that lead to complexity and unpredictability in tax systems which are consistent with the earlier academic research summarised above:

- *The desire to prevent tax avoidance:* the vicious cycle of complex anti-avoidance law interacts with an already complex system in ways which may not be fully appreciated in advance. Subsequent taxpayer circumvention requires even more complicated legislation.
- *The temptation to use tax to change society:* policymakers often try to make the latest change they want to society by using incentives and penalties in the tax system.
- *The need to 'do something':* the Chancellor always faces substantial cultural, political and legislative pressure to create some headlines on Budget day, so will fiddle with the tax system to do so.
- *The desire to pluck the goose without it hissing:*[7] policymakers often want, or need, to raise taxes but have long been afraid of raising headline rates of income tax. They thus resort to raising revenue in ways that (they believe) many people do not notice or understand, and thus add extra complexity to the system.

---

7   Jean-Baptiste Colbert, a finance minister to the French court in the seventeenth century, is reputed to have said that 'the art of taxation consists in so plucking the goose as to obtain the largest amount of feathers with the least possible amount of hissing'.

- *The problem of guarding the guardians:* because tax policy is now made and tested by HM Treasury, it does not receive the internal scrutiny that it should. This has led to poor policy and a greater likelihood of mistakes, thus undermining the trust in, and stability of, the tax system.[8]

In short, the UK tax system is in turmoil and there is a lack of trust on both sides. Practitioners and small businesses regard politicians and the Treasury as being out of touch with how businesses operate; equally, government and the tax authorities are suspicious of businesses, believing they will go to great lengths to avoid paying tax (Williams, 2008). The situation is set to continue spiralling as government continues to make incremental changes to the tax system without full consultation; sometimes to score quick political wins (which may subsequently turn into quick political own goals as in the introduction of the 10p starting rate of Income Tax and its subsequent removal) and sometimes as a knee-jerk reaction when they disagree with a court ruling (e.g. Arctic Systems). The lack of effective consultation only serves to further alienate the majority of taxpayers, who see the government jumping to the tune of those who shout loudest: for example, Capital Gains Tax simplification measures announced in PBR 2007 were subsequently amended following the outcry from certain sections of the population. All of this could have been avoided by a more measured approach with genuine consultation before the change was announced. The present system merely racks up the pages of legislation and contributes to the uncertainty faced by all taxpayers. These costs are borne most heavily by small businesses.

---

8   Policy used to be initiated by Inland Revenue and Customs and Excise, and reviewed by the Treasury.

Annexe

The ICAEW Tax Faculty's ten tenets for a better tax system

The tax system should be:

1. Statutory: tax legislation should be enacted by statute and subject to proper democratic scrutiny by Parliament.
2. Certain: in virtually all circumstances the application of the tax rules should be certain. It should not normally be necessary for anyone to resort to the courts in order to resolve how the rules operate in relation to his or her tax affairs.
3. Simple: the tax rules should aim to be simple, understandable and clear in their objectives.
4. Easy to collect and to calculate: a person's tax liability should be easy to calculate and straightforward and cheap to collect.
5. Properly targeted: when anti-avoidance legislation is passed, due regard should be paid to maintaining the simplicity and certainty of the tax system by targeting it to close specific loopholes.
6. Constant: Changes to the underlying rules should be kept to a minimum. There should be a justifiable economic and/or social basis for any change to the tax rules and this justification should be made public and the underlying policy made clear.
7. Subject to proper consultation: other than in exceptional circumstances, the government should allow adequate time for both the drafting of tax legislation and full consultation on it.
8. Regularly reviewed: the tax rules should be subject to a regular public review to determine their continuing relevance and whether their original justification has been realised. If a

tax rule is no longer relevant, then it should be repealed.
9. Fair and reasonable: the revenue authorities have a duty to exercise their powers reasonably. There should be a right of appeal to an independent tribunal against all their decisions.
10. Competitive: tax rules and rates should be framed so as to encourage investment, capital and trade in and with the UK.

These are explained in more detail in the discussion document published in October 1999 as TAXGUIDE 4/99.[9]

---

9   See http://www.icaew.com/index.cfm?route=118111.

7 TACKLING COMPLEXITY

Having identified that complexity is the main contributor to administrative and compliance costs, we now examine suggestions for tackling complexity. We note the following comment from the Meade Committee (Meade, 1978: 316): 'If all income (under an income tax regime) or all expenditure (under an expenditure tax regime) were subject to one single rate of tax, the administrative problems of the direct tax system could be simplified out of all recognition … [A]nd much complicated anti-avoidance legislation would become unnecessary.'

It is important to note that complexity in the system is not a new issue (references were made to complexity in Gladstone's time[1]), nor is it confined to the UK.

How to simplify the tax system: legislation and process

This is no easy task. Calls for simplification have increased,

---

1   In response to a demand in the House of Commons that tax law should be made intelligible to persons who had not received a legal education, Gladstone remarked in 1853 that the nature of property in the UK made it almost impossible to deal with Income Tax in a simple manner. Referring in 1981 to Gladstone's comments, the then Presiding Special Commissioner, Hubert Monroe, QC, suggested that it would be some advance if tax law were intelligible to those who *had* received a legal education (Budd, 2003: 14).

particularly during the period since Lord Howe's 1977[2] speech, but during the same period the volume and complexity of legislation have increased. Evans (2008: 5) describes this phenomenon:

> … [a] striking feature of the UK tax system over the past 30 years is the extent to which its principal stakeholders have been committed to the goal of simplification, combined with their failure to achieve any such simplification over the period. Indeed, many of the initiatives designed to simplify have only served to make that system, at its technical, operational and administrative levels, yet more complicated.

He reassures us that this is not unique to the UK, and is in fact a problem for most developed economies (see Chittenden and Foster, 2009: 26, for discussion of other countries).

In the UK it seems that a major barrier to change is that politics and tax policy are inextricably linked. Indeed, Riddell (2008: 16) is firmly of the view that: '… tax decisions cannot be taken out of politics. They are the stuff of the party battle'.

Riddell (ibid.) gives a number of insights into the tax policy decision-making of Chancellors Howe, Lawson, Clarke and Brown between 1979 and 2007, and illustrates that under the current system politicians view tax policy as fundamental to electoral success. It therefore seems unlikely that they will easily relinquish their grip.

Truman (2007) proposes that we need a radically different

---

2   Lord Howe acknowledges his lifelong interest in tax simplification, which he had spoken about even before he became Chancellor of the Exchequer in 1979. His 1977 address to the Addington Society (a group of the top tax professionals in the country which meets several times a year to consider the burning tax issues of the day) is among the best-known modern criticisms of Parliament's role in the process of creating tax law (Howe, 1977).

tax system, and that simplification on this scale would require the ongoing commitment of politicians and the government; thus it seems the most productive solution is likely to be a continuing process rather than a 'big bang' approach. This process would be two-pronged.

First, a model similar to that being used to reduce administrative burdens could be implemented with the express aim of reducing the volume of tax legislation by a set percentage in a specified time frame. The focus would be maintained by the efforts of a small number of senior people from the accountancy and legal professions and the government.

Second, once simplification has been achieved it is imperative to prevent Parliament reversing progress. Truman (ibid.) argues that one of the contributory factors is the UK legislative process with regard to direct taxes. Currently there is a need for an annual Finance Bill,[3] which must be passed by Parliament before the summer recess in order to guarantee the continued collection of taxes; therefore there is little time for effective scrutiny. This annual process creates an expectation that changes will be made every year when perhaps a cultural move away from this idea is called for. Truman recommends a slowing down of the legislative machinery by including more checks and balances; dispensing with the annual Finance Bill; and allowing the setting of tax rates by normal Budget resolutions. He suggests that tax bills will then

---

3   A relic from the history of UK taxation whereby Income Tax was introduced as a temporary tax in order to finance wars on a number of occasions and which Gladstone intended to phase out by 1860. 'Income tax is still a "temporary" tax – it expires each year on 5 April and Parliament has to reapply it by an annual Finance Act. For up to four months until the Finance Act becomes law, the Provisional Collection of Taxes Act 1913 ensures that taxes can still be demanded'; http://www.hmrc.gov.uk/history/taxhis2.htm, accessed 18 November 2008.

be required once every two or three years and that these should have to compete for parliamentary time like any other bill. Importantly, they should be heard by some kind of committee which is able to call on independent expert evidence.

This view is also expressed by Alt et al. (2008: 3), who believe that ensuring higher levels of pre-legislative scrutiny should be a priority for government; although they leave it open as to whether scrutiny of tax policy is best undertaken by the existing Treasury Select Committee or by a new select committee on taxation.

The ACCA, in their ten-point tax manifesto,[4] call for tax change to be driven by a Tax Policy Committee (TPC – see *Accountancy Age*, August 2000[5]), which they envisage would operate along the lines of the Monetary Policy Committee (MPC), in the same vein as a suggestion made by Broke (1999). Government would set the overall economic framework of the tax environment and the TPC would work on adjusting the tax system as appropriate, with a view to long-term simplification. Of course, to make this work, the TPC would need to be demonstrably independent in its stance.

As a final radical recommendation, Truman (2007) suggests that tax Bills should pass through the House of Lords as well as the Commons – currently this is not the case (the reason given is that the elected government must be able to raise the finances it needs for its planned expenditure). The removal of the requirement for an annual Finance Bill would, however, allow this further check to be reinstated.[6]

4   http://www.accaglobal.com/pubs/publicinterest/pressandpolicy/unit/manifestos/m4tax_manifesto.pdf.

5   http://www.accountancyage.com/accountancyage/comment/2037631/formulation-tax-legislation-endless-draft, accessed 21 November 2008.

6   'In 1909 Lloyd George introduced the first progressive tax on income in the

Practical changes to the current withholding arrangements

Shaw et al. (2008) suggested a number of changes to the current withholding arrangements to collect the correct amount of direct tax. These included:

- Development of an HMRC online computer coding system to reduce the amount of paper communication, e.g. HMRC sending tax codes to employees and P45s being taken by the employee from one employer to another.
- Making withholding other than PAYE (for example, with respect to interest income) non-flat-rate so that it was tailored to individual circumstances.
- Moving to monthly information reporting by employers – this may not be a significant additional burden on employers if the information is required in the same form as the year-end return. Naturally this would be easier in an electronic filing environment, and regard must be given to the position of small firms whose computer systems may not be so easily adapted.
- Universal self-assessment combined with simple non-cumulative withholding of taxes and pre-completion of returns.

Shaw et al. conclude (ibid.: 58): 'The question is whether it [the UK tax system] can adapt quickly enough. If not, it runs

so-called "People's Budget". The budget was not generally accepted and was rejected by the House of Lords in November 1909, but it eventually became law in 1910. As a result of this problem, the power of the House of Lords to veto budgets was removed in 1911 (and is still the case in the UK now)' (Lymer and Oats, 2008: 15).

the risk of imposing unnecessary burdens while simultaneously allowing revenues to escape taxation such that the tax burden is shared in a more capricious and inequitable fashion.'

Other issues are reviewed by Boys Smith et al. (2008). The current artificial segregation of income and inconsistent definitions (for example, between earnings for income taxes and NICs) across the different taxes faced by businesses result in a situation where all companies of whatever size have a constant need to review not only the accounting implications, but also, as a separate exercise, the tax implications of their business decisions. This results in costs not only in terms of the time of the business staff who deal with these issues, but also financially in terms of the advice sought from tax professionals. Further costs arise out of the distinction between accounting profits and profits for tax purposes: there is the cost of carrying out the necessary calculations (either by in-house staff or by a tax adviser) and also the cost of any tax planning undertaken to maximise the tax benefits due to differing treatments for tax purposes of, for example, business assets.

Other practical ways to simplify

A number of immediate changes to begin reversing tax complexity and thus reduce the economic burden are summarised by Boys Smith et al. (ibid.):

Accounting and tax profits

They argue that government should adopt the principle that the taxable profits of a business (whether operated by an individual or a company) should normally equal its accounting profits. An exception to this might be in the area of capital allowances if politicians want to be able to give incentives for investment.

Employed and self-employed taxation

They believe that policymakers should examine the differences in tax treatment of employed and self-employed and abolish any unjustified distinctions.

Capital and income

They suggest that the distinction between the two is not justified in many instances. Where it is, the government needs to make sure that it is sufficiently clear.

Reviewing reliefs

Policymakers should cut unnecessary reliefs and develop a way to make sure that new ones are not adopted when not needed. Principles could be established with which proposed targeted reliefs would need to comply. For example, such proposals should be subject to full impact assessment and consultation, including with tax advisers; the uptake and processing should be tested through a small-scale pilot; reliefs should be part of a wider programme to promote change, such as an information campaign; the introduction of targeted reliefs should be supported by organisational arrangements within HMRC to ensure consistency and speed in handling of applications, etc.

Further areas for review

The government, argue Boys Smith et al., should consider simplifying distinctions made on supplies of goods or services for VAT purposes, rather than spending taxpayers' money on convoluted discussions and court cases to settle whether a Pringle is a crisp or a Jaffa cake a cake. It is difficult to justify the complexity arising as a result of these less than obvious distinctions.

They also argue that the rules for calculating National Insurance Contributions are complicated and needlessly distinct from the rules for calculating Income Tax. The Institute for Fiscal Studies (IFS) is undertaking a review into the practicalities of integrating Income Tax and National Insurance and the interim report (Adam and Loutzenhiser, 2007) concludes that although there are potential benefits from integration, merely merging the two would result in a situation so complicated that it might nullify the benefits of integration. They suggest that significant reform of the policy framework is required, and their view is that this would entail significant transition costs. They promise recommendations for reform. We suggest that the definitions and rules for calculating NICs and Income Tax should be aligned. It may be that NICs should be abolished altogether, perhaps with raised personal allowances for retired persons living on savings.[7]

A number of other suggestions are made by Boys Smith et al., including distinguishing between business and non-business profits for tax purposes rather than using different tax schedules; the rationalisation of the taxation of savings vehicles; the reform of Stamp Duty; the integration of tax credits into the tax

---

7   If Income Tax rates were raised and NICs abolished, then those who do not pay Income Tax, such as those above state pension age, would have an increased tax burden.

system and the reform of the imputation system for the taxing of dividends.

A further issue is to review those taxes where the revenue is minimal but there are high administrative and compliance costs, such as Capital Gains Tax and Inheritance Tax. It may make sense to abolish these (see Myddelton, 1994: 94).

The role of advisers in enabling government to administer taxes efficiently

A recent report (BRE, 2007) finds that: 'Businesses spend at least £1.4 billion each year on advice to help them comply with regulation. Businesses will pay for advice if they feel that this is cheaper or easier than following regulations on their own.'

The report includes an estimate of the total market for accountancy, legal and employment services in the UK as exceeding £23 billion, a proportion of which relates to tax compliance. Recommendations are made for making real reductions in the amount businesses need to spend on regulatory advice by tackling the five drivers of advice identified in this report; these are:

- Volume and complexity.
- Low awareness of government guidance.
- Regulatory change.
- Poor-quality government guidance.
- Uncertainty, risk and lack of confidence.

In general terms, it can be seen from the previous discussion that these would apply equally to tax legislation.

The BRE suggest that by taking action to reduce the effects of these drivers government can reduce the overall costs businesses face in following regulations. They claim that the recommendations in their report would make a real difference to the experience of regulation for businesses, and that actions delivering even a 5 per cent reduction in the lowest estimate of the size of the market for business advice on regulation would give a mean reduction in business spending of more than £72 million (ibid.: 8).

Even if significant progress is made on tackling the five drivers of advice there will still be a role for business advisers in the delivery of regulation. Economies of scale mean it is often more efficient for a single business adviser to gain a detailed understanding of a complex area of regulation and sell this on to businesses than for each business to learn about the regulations for itself.

The fact that there will therefore always be a role for intermediaries in advising on regulation should not obscure the fact that the market for regulatory advice is a market that is the product of the way government designs and implements regulation. There are areas of regulation where businesses would need less advice if the design and delivery of regulation were improved.

The overall recommendations in the BRE report for the regulatory process in general, many of which are equally relevant to tax policy, are as follows:

Improving the regulatory process

- Plan guidance at an early stage of the policy process.
- Issue guidance earlier.

Improving communication on regulation

- Increase the market penetration of www.businesslink.gov.uk.
- Communicate directly with businesses using high-quality, simple guidance.
- Communicate with businesses through intermediaries.

Improving the quality of government advice on regulation

- Improve feedback mechanisms on guidance.
- Consider joint-badging or outsourcing the design of guidance.

Improving the environment for business advice on regulation

- Help businesses become informed consumers of advice services by increasing understanding of regulatory requirements.
- Take advantage of online forums for businesses to share information on regulations.
- Provide dedicated guidance for advisers where appropriate.

An agenda for change

We have seen in previous chapters that the chief contributory factor to the increasing hidden costs of taxation is complexity, both in tax legislation and in the workings of the tax system. In this chapter, we have examined the work of other authors who have proposed changes that will reduce the burden on business of compliance with the tax system. We now summarise the changes that we believe need to be made to substantially reduce compliance costs, and the distortions they create. The drivers of complexity are:

- The weight of past legislation.
- The desire to prevent tax avoidance.
- The temptation to use tax to change society.
- The pressure on the Chancellor to 'do something' on an annual basis.
- The desire to raise taxes in a way that will be less obvious to the taxpayer (and thus minimise the outcry by lobbying factions).
- The lack of scrutiny before tax policy is enacted, leading to mistakes and lack of stability and trust in the tax system (if not the political process as a whole).

To reduce complexity and operating costs, the following broad areas should be addressed.

Major simplification of the existing legislation

The tax law rewrite project should be expanded with a view to much larger-scale simplification of tax legislation. It should be an ongoing process similar in nature to the administrative burdens reduction programme, requiring buy-in from government and politicians with the setting of targets for quantified reductions in the tax code to be achieved within a specific time frame. As noted in the previous chapter, we also believe that true progress can be made only if new legislation is formatted in the tax law rewrite style from the outset. There should be a review of the current legislation, carried out by specialists reporting to a multiparty, multidisciplinary advisory board. Once this has been achieved, any proposed changes should be subject to a defined process prior to enactment in order to identify any anomalies before they reach the statute book.

The legislative process

The circus of the annual Finance Act should cease. Instead, the government should be required to submit a statement of its tax and fiscal policy for a three- to five-year period, with rates to be set by normal Budget resolutions, and tax Bills every two or three years. This will help halt the annual increase in complexity by allowing more scrutiny to ensure a coherent overall structure for taxation, with the Budget resolutions simply setting the rates within this structure. More effective pre-legislative scrutiny of tax policy could involve bodies such as ACCA, CIOT and ICAEW, which have made representations on this issue.

Reducing complexity in business taxes

The authors concur with the recommendations summarised by Boys Smith et al.:

- Alignment of accounting and taxable profits: the government should adopt the principle that the taxable profits of a business (whether operated by an individual or a company) should normally equal its accounting profits. To illustrate this, the whole area of assets used in a business should be examined with a view to removing distinctions between, and giving consistent treatment to, fundamentally similar items, such as hire purchase contracts and finance leases. Similarly, the area of capital allowances versus accounting depreciation is another area for simplification.
- Employed and self-employed taxation: policymakers should look at the differences in tax treatment and abolish any distinctions that do not have a strong justification. As

previously discussed by Crawford and Freedman (2008: 28), the tax system should treat all taxpayers equally. The present system only encourages the distortion of commercial decision-making. The differential NIC treatment of employees and the self-employed is an example of this.

- Capital and income: the distinction between the two is not justified in many instances. Where it is, the government needs to make sure that it is sufficiently clear. Indeed, a case can be made for abolishing or limiting Capital Gains Tax to very specific circumstances. Investment returns that are disguised as capital gains should be taxed in the same way that income is taxed. This would reduce the tendency to engineer financial instruments to avoid tax on income.
- Reviewing reliefs: policymakers should cut unnecessary reliefs and develop a way to make sure that new ones are not adopted when not needed. Tax reliefs are really a form of government planning or picking winners – it is believed that economic outcomes will improve if certain forms of economic behaviour are treated relatively favourably by the tax system. A considerable reduction in the availability of reliefs will come about only if there is a change in government philosophy about government's ability to pick business 'winners'.

General recommendations

In addition, we have a number of general recommendations for future tax policy.

- The use of common definitions and procedures across taxes

reduces costs by decreasing the number of calculations that have to be made. Therefore we recommend that there should be consistency of definitions and procedures across all taxes. The obvious example that springs to mind here is the case of Income Tax and National Insurance. For several years now, many have been calling for an alignment of the rules for calculating Income Tax and National Insurance. As a minimum, remuneration packages should attract the same amount of tax and National Insurance no matter how they are structured.

- We suggest a review of those taxes which generate minimal revenue in return for high administrative and compliance costs, such as Capital Gains Tax and Inheritance Tax. It might be better if these taxes were scrapped completely.
- Where compliance costs represent a burden that cannot be reduced, government and the tax authorities should consider compensation for the costs incurred.

Taken as a whole the proposals made in this document are radical, especially the proposed move from annual Finance Acts to a more stable fiscal policy that would emerge from rigorous analysis and consideration of fiscal needs rather than the pressure for Chancellors of all political persuasions to 'pull rabbits from the hat' in each Budget speech. As we have argued above, studies of the costs of complying with tax laws and regulations indicate that it is the need for businesses to adapt to continual change and to cope with complexity arising from the volume of laws and regulations which is responsible for the majority of compliance costs; the same must be true for HMRC. Consequently a more stable tax regime subject to fewer changes will be much less burdensome on the private sector of the economy and on government. Acknowledgement that, in the current economic circumstances, a figure equivalent to 3p to 4p on the basic rate of Income Tax is currently absorbed by the hidden costs of taxation indicates the scale of the savings that could be made. More careful political and administrative management of taxes could surely release between one quarter and one third of these costs.

REFERENCES

Accountancy Age (2008), 'UK loses ranking as favourable tax regime', 10 October, http://www.accountancyage.com/accountancyage/news/2227970/uk-loses-ranking-favourable, accessed 10 October 2008.

Adam, S. and J. Browne (2009), *A Survey of the UK Tax System*, Institute for Fiscal Studies, Briefing Note no. 9, April.

Adam, S. and G. Loutzenhiser (2007), *Integrating Income Tax and National Insurance: An interim report*, IFS Working Papers W07/21, December.

Alt, J., I. Preston and L. Sibieta (2008), *The Political Economy of Tax Policy*, Mirrlees Review, Institute for Fiscal Studies, available at www.ifs.org.uk/mirrleesreview/publications. php, last accessed 14 September 2008.

Ambler, T., F. Chittenden and C. Hwang (2005), *Regulation: Another Form of Taxation? UK Regulatory Impact Assessments in 2003/04*, London: BCC.

Ambler, T., F. Chittenden and S. Iancich (2008), *The UK Regulatory System*, British Chambers of Commerce, March, available at http://www.britishchambers.org.uk/6798219243315023264/regulation.html, last accessed 4 December 2008.

ATAX (1997), 'A report into the taxpayer costs of compliance', Australian Tax Office.

Bannock, G. (2005), 'Government regulation: an overview', in G. Bannock and C. Gray (eds), *Government Regulation and the Small Firm*, Milton Keynes: Institute for Small Business and Entrepreneurship, Small Enterprise Research Team, pp. 15–26.

Bartlett, B. (1994), 'How excessive government killed Ancient Rome', *Cato Journal*, 14(2).

Bennett, F., M. Brewer and J. Shaw (2009), *Understanding the Compliance Costs of Benefits and Tax Credits*, Institute for Fiscal Studies, July.

Blackburn, R. A., M. Hart, D. Smallbone, J. Kitching, W. Eadson and K. Bannon (2005), *Analysis of the Impact of the Tax System on the Cash Flow of Small Businesses: A Report for HM Revenue and Customs (HMRC)*, Kingston Business School.

Blunden, G. H. (1892), 'The position and function of the Income Tax in the British fiscal system', *Economic Journal*, 2(8): 637–52.

Bolton, J. E. (1971), 'Small firms: report of the Committee of Inquiry on Small Firms', Cmnd 4811, London: HMSO.

Boys Smith, N., D. Martin and L. Kay (2008), *The Cost of Complexity*, available at http://www.policyexchange.org.uk/ Publications.aspx?id=750, last accessed 7 November 2008.

BRE (Better Regulation Executive) (2005), *Measuring Administrative Costs: UK Standard Cost Model Manual*, London: Cabinet Office.

BRE (2007), *Regulation and Business Advice*, London: Department for Business, Enterprise and Regulatory Reform.

Broke, A. (1999), *Simplification of Tax or I Wouldn't Start from Here*, ICAEW Tax Faculty Hardman Lecture, available at http://www.icaew.com/index.cfm/route/158041/icaew_ga/en/Home/pdf, accessed 8 December 2008.

BRTF (Better Regulation Task Force) (2005), *Regulation – Less Is More: Reducing Burdens, Improving Outcomes*, London, March.

Budd, A. (2003), *Making Tax Law, Report of a Working Party on the Institutional Processes for the Parliamentary Scrutiny of Tax Proposals and for the Enactment of Tax Legislation*, TLRC Discussion Paper no. 3, Tax Law Review Committee, London: IFS.

Chittenden, F. and H. Foster (2008a), 'Fairness in the taxation of small businesses', in C. Wales (ed.) (2008), *Fair Tax: Towards a modern tax system*, London: The Smith Institute, pp. 27–40.

Chittenden, F. and H. Foster (2008b), *Perspectives on Fair Tax*, London: ACCA.

Chittenden, F. and H. Foster (2009), *Is There a Way out of the Tax Labyrinth?*, London: ACCA, available at http://www.accaglobal.com/pubs/general/activities/library/other_issues/other_pubs/2009/tech-tp-tl.pdf, accessed 12 June 2009.

Chittenden, F. and B. Sloan (2007), 'Quantifying inequity in the taxation of individuals and small firms', *British Tax Review*, 1: 58–72.

Chittenden, F., S. Kauser and P. Poutziouris (2002), *The Regulatory Burdens of Small Business: A Literature Review*, available at http://www.berr.gov.uk/files/file38324.pdf, accessed 30 July 2008.

Chittenden, F., S. Kauser and P. Poutziouris (2003), 'Tax regulation and small business in the USA, UK, Australia &

New Zealand', *International Small Business Journal*, 21(1): 93–115.

Chittenden, F., S. Kauser and P. Poutziouris (2005), 'PAYE-NIC compliance costs, empirical evidence from the UK economy', *International Small Business Journal*, 23(6): 635–56.

Chittenden, F., P. Poutziouris, S. Kauser and M. Shamutkova (2005), 'Income Tax Self-Assessment compliance costs: empirical evidence from the UK', in G. Bannock and C. Gray (eds), *Government Regulation and the Small Firm*, Milton Keynes: Institute for Small Business and Entrepreneurship, Small Enterprise Research Team, pp. 27–38.

Chittenden, F., P. Poutziouris, N. Michaelas and T. Watts (1999a), 'Taxation and small firms: creating incentives for the reinvestment of profits', *Environment and Planning C: Government and Policy*, 17(3): 271–86.

Chittenden, F., P. Poutziouris, N. Michaelas and T. Watts (1999b), 'Modelling the impact of taxation on the small-business economy: the NatWest/MBS Tax Index for the self-employed, sole-traders, and partnerships', *Environment and Planning C: Government and Policy*, 17(5): 577–92.

Crawford, C. and J. Freedman (2008), *Small Business Taxation: A special study of the structural issues surrounding the taxation of business profits of owner managed firms undertaken for the Mirrlees Review*, available at http://www.ifs.org.uk/ mirrleesreview/press_docs/small_businesses.pdf, accessed 3 September 2008.

Dennis, A. and B. Shepherd (2007), *Trade Costs, Barriers to Entry, and Export Diversification in Developing Countries*, Washington, DC: World Bank.

DWP (2006), *Security in Retirement: Towards a New Pensions System*, Government White Paper Cm 6841, May, available at www.dwp.gov.uk/pensionsreform, accessed 8 October 2008.

Erard, B. and J. S. Feinstein (1994), 'Honesty and evasion in the tax compliance game', *RAND Journal of Economics*, 25(1): 1–19.

European Commission (2007), *Simplified Tax Compliance Procedures for SMEs: Final Report of the Expert Group*, June.

Evans, C. (2001), 'The operating costs of taxation: A review of the research', *Economic Affairs*, 21(2): 5–9.

Evans, C. (2003a), 'Studying the studies: an overview of recent research into taxation operating costs', *eJournal of Tax Research*, 1(1): 64–92.

Evans, C. (2003b), *Taxing Personal Capital Gains: Operating Cost Implications*, Research Study no. 40, Australian Tax Research Foundation.

Evans, C. (2008), *Taxation in the UK: Commentary*, Mirrlees Review, Institute for Fiscal Studies, available at http://www.ifs.org.uk/mirrleesreview/publications.php, accessed 20 January 2009.

Evans, C. J., J. Hasseldine and J. Pope (2001), 'State of the art and future directions' in C. J. Evans, J. Pope and J. Hasseldine (eds), *Tax Compliance Costs: A Festschrift for Cedric Sandford*, Australia: Prospect Media Pty Ltd.

Faith, J. (2008), 'EU ministers reach agreement on fight against VAT fraud', available at http://www.internationaltaxreview.com/?Page=9&PUBID=210&ISS=25166&SID=714227, accessed 5 December 2008.

Freedman, J. (2008), 'Where do we go from here?', *Tax Adviser*, London: Chartered Institute of Taxation, June.

Gordon, K. M. (2009), 'The right amount of tax', *Weekly Tax News*, 553, 6 July.

Graetz, M. J. (2005), 'A fair and balanced tax system for the twenty-first century', in A. J. Auerback and K. A. Hassett (eds), *Toward Fundamental Tax Reform*, Washington, DC: AEI Press, pp. 48–69.

Haig, R. M. (1935), 'The cost to business concerns of compliance with tax laws', *Management Review*, 54: 232–333.

Hansford, A., J. Hasseldine and C. Howorth (2003), 'Factors affecting the costs of UK VAT compliance for Small and Medium-Sized Enterprises', *Environment and Planning C: Government and Policy*, 21: 479–92.

Hasseldine, J. (2001), 'Linkages between compliance costs and taxpayer compliance research', in C. J. Evans, J. Pope and J. Hasseldine (eds), *Tax Compliance Costs: A Festschrift for Cedric Sandford*, Australia: Prospect Media Pty Ltd.

Highfield, R. (2008), 'Tax implementations', Commentary on S. Shaw, J. Slemrod and J. Whiting, 'Administration and compliance', Chapter 12 in Mirrlees Review.

HM Treasury (2007), *VAT Simplification Review: Update*, December.

HMRC (2008a), *Delivering a New Relationship with Business: Progress on HMRC's plans to improve the SME customer experience*, March, http://www.hmrc.gov.uk/budget2008/delivering-new-relationship.pdf, accessed 17 October 2008.

HMRC (2008b), *The Framework for a Better Relationship: Making a difference: review of links with large business*, http://www.hmrc.gov.uk/budget2008/framework-better-relations.pdf, accessed 17 October 2008.

Holtz-Eakin, D. (1995), 'Should small businesses be tax favoured?', *National Tax Journal*, 48(3): 387–95.

Holtz-Eakin, D. (2000), 'Public policy toward entrepreneurship', *Small Business Economics*, 15(4): 283–91.

House of Commons Treasury Committee (2004), *The Administrative Costs of Tax Compliance*, 7th Report of Session 2003–04, HC 269, London.

Howe, Sir Geoffrey (1977), 'Reform of taxation machinery', *British Tax Review*, 2: 97–104.

Howe, Sir Geoffrey (2000), *Simplicity and Stability: The Politics of Tax Policy*, available at http://www.icaew.com/index.cfm/ route/133415, accessed 15 December 2008.

Hurwich, D. (2001), 'Tax avoidance discussed', *Tax Adviser*, September; see Chartered Institute of Taxation website: http://www.tax.org.uk/showarticle.pl?id=491&n=379, accessed 9 March 2008.

Inland Revenue (1998), *The Tax Compliance Costs for Employers of PAYE and National Insurance in 1995–96*, Centre for Fiscal Studies, University of Bath.

Johnson, S. (1990), 'Small firms policies: an agenda for the 1990s', in M. Robertson, E. Chell and C. Mason, *Towards the 21st Century: The Challenge for Small Business*, Macclesfield: Nadamal Books, pp. 12–29.

Johnston, K. S. (1961), *Corporations' Federal Income Tax Compliance Costs*, Monograph No. 10, Ohio State University Bureau of Business Research.

Kauser, S., F. Chittenden and P. Poutziouris (2001), *On the VAT Affairs of Small Firms: Empirical evidence from the UK SME economy*, Paper presented at the 24th ISBA National Small Firms Conference: Exploring the Frontiers of Small Business,

Leicester; Manchester: Business Development Centre, Manchester Business School, University of Manchester.

Kauser, S., F. Chittenden, P. Poutziouris and B. Sloan (2005), 'Corporation Tax Self-Assessment compliance costs: empirical evidence from the UK', in G. Bannock and C. Gray (eds), *Government Regulation and the Small Firm*, Milton Keynes: Institute for Small Business and Entrepreneurship, Small Enterprise Research Team, pp. 15–26.

KPMG LLP (2006), *Administrative Burdens – HMRC Measurement Project*, London, http://www.hmrc.gov.uk/better-regulation/kpmg.htm, accessed 21 August 2008.

LBRO (Local Better Regulation Office) (2008), *Regulatory Reform at Local Level: Prosperity and Protection*, Conference, London, 18 September.

Lewis, A. (1982), *The Psychology of Taxation*, New York: St Martin's Press.

Lindsay, C. and C. Macaulay (2004), 'Growth in self-employment in the UK', *Labour Market Trends*, Office of National Statistics, October, pp. 399–404.

Lymer, A. and L. Oats (2008), *Taxation Policy and Practice*, 14th edn, Birmingham: Fiscal Publications.

Martin, J. W. (1944), 'Cost of tax administration, examples of compliance expenses', *Bulletin of the National Tax Association*, April, pp. 194–205.

Meade, J. E. (1978), *The Structure and Reform of Direct Taxation*, London: Institute for Fiscal Studies, available at http://www.ifs.org.uk/docs/meade.pdf, accessed 17 July 2009.

Müller, F. J. (1963), *The Burden of Compliance*, Seattle Bureau of Business Research.

Myddelton, D. R. (1994), *The Power to Destroy: A Study of the British Tax System*, London: Society for Individual Freedom.

NAO (National Audit Office) (2007), *HM Revenue & Customs 2006–07 Accounts: The Comptroller and Auditor General's Standard Report*, London: NAO.

Nellis, J. G. and D. Parker (1996), *The Essence of the Economy*, 2nd edn, Prentice Hall.

OECD (2006), *Consumption Tax Trends, VAT/GST and Excise Rates, Trends and Administration Issues*, Paris.

OECD (2007), *Tax Administration in OECD Countries and Selected Non-OECD Countries: Comparative Information Series (2006)*, Centre for Tax Policy and Administration (CTPA).

OECD (2008), Forum on Tax Administration: Taxpayer Services Sub-Group, CTPA.

OECD (2009), *Tax Administration in OECD Countries and Selected Non-OECD Countries: Comparative Information Series (2008)*, CTPA.

Peat Marwick (1985), 'A comparative analysis of sales tax compliance costs for retail businesses', Mimeo, Washington, DC: Small Business Administration.

Pitt, M. M. and J. R. Slemrod (1988), 'The compliance costs of itemising deductions: evidence from individual tax returns', Mimeo.

Pope, J. (1992), 'The compliance costs of taxation in Australia: an economic and policy perspective', School of Economics and Finance Working Paper 92.07, Curtin University, Perth.

Pope, J., R. Fayle and D. L. Chen (1991), *The Compliance Costs of Public Companies' Income Taxation in Australia 1986/87*, Sydney: Australia Tax Research Foundation.

PwC (2007), *Paying Taxes: The Global Picture*, London: PricewaterhouseCoopers/World Bank.

Redston, A. (2004), 'Small business in the eye of the storm', *British Tax Review*, 5: 566–81.

Rice, P. (2001), 'The UK approach to compliance cost assessment of tax changes – the development of regulatory impact assessments in the UK', in C. J. Evans, J. Pope and J. Hasseldine (eds), *Tax Compliance Costs: A Festschrift for Cedric Sandford*, Australia: Prospect Media Pty Ltd.

Riddell, P. (2008), *The Political Economy of Tax Policy: Commentary*, Mirrlees Review, Institute for Fiscal Studies, available at http://www.ifs.org.uk/mirrleesreview/publications.php, accessed 20 January 2009.

Sandford, C. (1973), *Hidden Costs of Taxation*, Institute for Fiscal Studies, Publication no. 6, July.

Sandford, C. (1995), *Tax Compliance Costs Measurement and Policy*, Fiscal Publications in association wth the Institute for Fiscal Studies.

Sandford, C. T., M. R. Godwin and P. J. W. Hardwick (1989), *Administrative and Compliance Costs of Taxation*, London: Fiscal Publications.

Sandford, C. T., M. R. Godwin, P. J. W. Hardwick and M. I. Butterworth (1981), *Cost and Benefits of VAT*, London: Heinemann.

SBRT (Small Business Research Trust) (1996), 'NatWest SBRT quarterly survey of small businesses in Britain', *SBRT*, 12(1).

SBRT (1998), 'NatWest SBRT quarterly survey of small businesses in Britain', *SBRT*, 14(1).

SERT (Small Enterprise Research Team) (2007), *Quarterly Survey of Small Business in Britain*, available at http://www.serteam.

co.uk/index.asp?contentid=38&menuid=1: NatWest_
SERTeam_Q2_2007_highlights.pdf.

Shaw, J., J. Slemrod and J. Whiting (2008), *Administration and Compliance*, Mirrlees Review, Institute for Fiscal Studies, available at www.ifs.org.uk/mirrleesreview/publications. php, last accessed 14 September 2008.

Sloan, B. (2007), 'Determining the incidence of direct taxation on the United Kingdom small and medium-sized enterprise sector', Unpublished PhD thesis, University of Manchester.

Sloan, B. and F. Chittenden (2006), 'Targeting fiscal policy to promote business growth amongst the self-employed', *Environment and Planning C: Government and Policy*, 24(1): 83–98.

Smith, A. (1776), *An Inquiry into the Nature and Causes of the Wealth of Nations*, Ward Lock & Co. (World Library 1812 reprint).

Strümpel, B. (1966), 'The disguised tax burden', *National Tax Journal*, 19(1): 70–77.

Thexton, M. (2008), 'Crazy horses', *Taxation*, 162(4175): 340–42.

Tran-Nam, B., C. Evans, M. Walpole and K. Ritchie (2000), 'Tax compliance costs: research methodology and empirical evidence from Australia', *National Tax Journal*, 53(2): 229–52.

Truman, M. (2007), *Slowing the Machine*, Hardman Memorial Lecture, ICAEW Tax Faculty, available at http://www.icaew. com/index.cfm/route/152623/icaew_ga/pdf, accessed 5 December 2008.

Truman, M. (2008), 'Faultlines', *Taxation*, 162(4175): 315–17.

Vaillancourt, F. (1989), 'The administrative and compliance costs of personal income taxes and payroll taxes, Canada, 1986', Canadian Tax Foundation.

Walpole, M., C. Evans, K. Ritchie and B. Tran-Nam (1999), 'Tax compliance costs: some lessons from "down under"', *British Tax Review*, 4: 244–71.

Whiting J. (2003), 'Employment taxes: Where are we going?', *Economic Affairs*, 23(1): 11–16.

Williams, P. (2008), *Policy? What Policy?*, http://www.accaglobal. com/members/publications/accounting_business/ archive/2008/april/3085262, accessed 20 November 2008.

Woellner, R., C. Coleman, M. McKerchar, M. Walpole and J. Zetler (2001), 'Taxation or vexation – measuring the psychological costs of tax compliance', in C. J. Evans, J. Pope and J. Hasseldine (eds), *Tax Compliance Costs: A Festschrift for Cedric Sandford*, Australia: Prospect Media Pty Ltd.

World Bank (2003), *Doing Business 2004: Understanding Regulation*, Washington, DC: World Bank.

World Bank (2004), *Doing Business 2005: Removing Obstacles to Growth*, Washington, DC: World Bank.

World Bank (2005), *Doing Business 2006: Creating Jobs*, Washington, DC: World Bank.

World Bank (2006), *Doing Business 2007: How to Reform*, Washington, DC: World Bank.

World Bank (2007), *Doing Business 2008*, Washington, DC: World Bank.

World Bank (2008), *Doing Business 2009*, Washington, DC: World Bank.

World Bank (2009), *Doing Business 2010, Overview*, Washington, DC: World Bank.

Yocum, J. C. (1961), *Retailers' Costs of Sales Tax Collection in Ohio*, Ohio State University Bureau of Business Research.

Young, J. C. (1994), 'Factors associated with non-compliance: evidence from the Michigan Tax Amnesty Program', *Journal of the American Taxation Association*, 16(2): 82–105.

ABOUT THE IEA

The Institute is a research and educational charity (No. CC 235 351), limited by guarantee. Its mission is to improve understanding of the fundamental institutions of a free society by analysing and expounding the role of markets in solving economic and social problems.

The IEA achieves its mission by:

- a high-quality publishing programme
- conferences, seminars, lectures and other events
- outreach to school and college students
- brokering media introductions and appearances

The IEA, which was established in 1955 by the late Sir Antony Fisher, is an educational charity, not a political organisation. It is independent of any political party or group and does not carry on activities intended to affect support for any political party or candidate in any election or referendum, or at any other time. It is financed by sales of publications, conference fees and voluntary donations.

In addition to its main series of publications the IEA also publishes a quarterly journal, *Economic Affairs*.

The IEA is aided in its work by a distinguished international Academic Advisory Council and an eminent panel of Honorary Fellows. Together with other academics, they review prospective IEA publications, their comments being passed on anonymously to authors. All IEA papers are therefore subject to the same rigorous independent refereeing process as used by leading academic journals.

IEA publications enjoy widespread classroom use and course adoptions in schools and universities. They are also sold throughout the world and often translated/reprinted.

Since 1974 the IEA has helped to create a worldwide network of 100 similar institutions in over 70 countries. They are all independent but share the IEA's mission.

Views expressed in the IEA's publications are those of the authors, not those of the Institute (which has no corporate view), its Managing Trustees, Academic Advisory Council members or senior staff.

Members of the Institute's Academic Advisory Council, Honorary Fellows, Trustees and Staff are listed on the following page.

The Institute gratefully acknowledges financial support for its publications programme and other work from a generous benefaction by the late Alec and Beryl Warren.

167

Other papers recently published by the IEA include:

A Market in Airport Slots
Keith Boyfield (editor), David Starkie, Tom Bass & Barry Humphreys
Readings 56; ISBN 0 255 36505 5; £10.00

Money, Inflation and the Constitutional Position of the Central Bank
Milton Friedman & Charles A. E. Goodhart
Readings 57; ISBN 0 255 36538 1; £10.00

railway.com
Parallels between the Early British Railways and the ICT Revolution
Robert C. B. Miller
Research Monograph 57; ISBN 0 255 36534 9; £12.50

The Regulation of Financial Markets
Edited by Philip Booth & David Currie
Readings 58; ISBN 0 255 36551 9; £12.50

Climate Alarmism Reconsidered
Robert L. Bradley Jr
Hobart Paper 146; ISBN 0 255 36541 1; £12.50

Government Failure: E. G. West on Education
Edited by James Tooley & James Stanfield
Occasional Paper 130; ISBN 0 255 36552 7; £12.50

Corporate Governance: Accountability in the Marketplace
Elaine Sternberg
Second edition
Hobart Paper 147; ISBN 0 255 36542 X; £12.50

The Land Use Planning System
Evaluating Options for Reform
John Corkindale
Hobart Paper 148; ISBN 0 255 36550 0; £10.00

Economy and Virtue
Essays on the Theme of Markets and Morality
Edited by Dennis O'Keeffe
Readings 59; ISBN 0 255 36504 7; £12.50

Free Markets Under Siege
Cartels, Politics and Social Welfare
Richard A. Epstein
Occasional Paper 132; ISBN 0 255 36553 5; £10.00

Unshackling Accountants
D. R. Myddelton
Hobart Paper 149; ISBN 0 255 36559 4; £12.50

The Euro as Politics
Pedro Schwartz
Research Monograph 58; ISBN 0 255 36535 7; £12.50

Pricing Our Roads
Vision and Reality
Stephen Glaister & Daniel J. Graham
Research Monograph 59; ISBN 0 255 36562 4; £10.00

The Role of Business in the Modern World
Progress, Pressures, and Prospects for the Market Economy
David Henderson
Hobart Paper 150; ISBN 0 255 36548 9; £12.50

Public Service Broadcasting Without the BBC?
Alan Peacock
Occasional Paper 133; ISBN 0 255 36565 9; £10.00

The ECB and the Euro: the First Five Years
Otmar Issing
Occasional Paper 134; ISBN 0 255 36555 1; £10.00

Towards a Liberal Utopia?
Edited by Philip Booth
Hobart Paperback 32; ISBN 0 255 36563 2; £15.00

The Way Out of the Pensions Quagmire
Philip Booth & Deborah Cooper
Research Monograph 60; ISBN 0 255 36517 9; £12.50

Black Wednesday
A Re-examination of Britain's Experience in the Exchange Rate Mechanism
Alan Budd
Occasional Paper 135; ISBN 0 255 36566 7; £7.50

Crime: Economic Incentives and Social Networks
Paul Ormerod
Hobart Paper 151; ISBN 0 255 36554 3; £10.00

The Road to Serfdom *with* **The Intellectuals and Socialism**
Friedrich A. Hayek
Occasional Paper 136; ISBN 0 255 36576 4; £10.00

Money and Asset Prices in Boom and Bust
Tim Congdon
Hobart Paper 152; ISBN 0 255 36570 5; £10.00

The Dangers of Bus Re-regulation
and Other Perspectives on Markets in Transport
John Hibbs et al.
Occasional Paper 137; ISBN 0 255 36572 1; £10.00

The New Rural Economy
Change, Dynamism and Government Policy
Berkeley Hill et al.
Occasional Paper 138; ISBN 0 255 36546 2; £15.00

The Benefits of Tax Competition
Richard Teather
Hobart Paper 153; ISBN 0 255 36569 1; £12.50

Wheels of Fortune
Self-funding Infrastructure and the Free Market Case for a Land Tax
Fred Harrison
Hobart Paper 154; ISBN 0 255 36589 6; £12.50

Were 364 Economists All Wrong?
Edited by Philip Booth
Readings 60; ISBN 978 0 255 36588 8; £10.00

Europe After the 'No' Votes
Mapping a New Economic Path
Patrick A. Messerlin
Occasional Paper 139; ISBN 978 0 255 36580 2; £10.00

The Railways, the Market and the Government
John Hibbs et al.
Readings 61; ISBN 978 0 255 36567 3; £12.50

Corruption: The World's Big C
Cases, Causes, Consequences, Cures
Ian Senior
Research Monograph 61; ISBN 978 0 255 36571 0; £12.50

Choice and the End of Social Housing
Peter King
Hobart Paper 155; ISBN 978 0 255 36568 0; £10.00

Sir Humphrey's Legacy
Facing Up to the Cost of Public Sector Pensions
Neil Record
Hobart Paper 156; ISBN 978 0 255 36578 9; £10.00

The Economics of Law
Cento Veljanovski
Second edition
Hobart Paper 157; ISBN 978 0 255 36561 1; £12.50

Living with Leviathan
Public Spending, Taxes and Economic Performance
David B. Smith
Hobart Paper 158; ISBN 978 0 255 36579 6; £12.50

The Vote Motive
Gordon Tullock
New edition
Hobart Paperback 33; ISBN 978 0 255 36577 2; £10.00

Waging the War of Ideas
John Blundell
Third edition
Occasional Paper 131; ISBN 978 0 255 36606 9; £12.50

The War Between the State and the Family
How Government Divides and Impoverishes
Patricia Morgan
Hobart Paper 159; ISBN 978 0 255 36596 3; £10.00

Capitalism – A Condensed Version
Arthur Seldon
Occasional Paper 140; ISBN 978 0 255 36598 7; £7.50

Catholic Social Teaching and the Market Economy
Edited by Philip Booth
Hobart Paperback 34; ISBN 978 0 255 36581 9; £15.00

Adam Smith – A Primer
Eamonn Butler
Occasional Paper 141; ISBN 978 0 255 36608 3; £7.50

Happiness, Economics and Public Policy
Helen Johns & Paul Ormerod
Research Monograph 62; ISBN 978 0 255 36600 7; £10.00

They Meant Well
Government Project Disasters
D. R. Myddelton
Hobart Paper 160; ISBN 978 0 255 36601 4; £12.50

Rescuing Social Capital from Social Democracy
John Meadowcroft & Mark Pennington
Hobart Paper 161; ISBN 978 0 255 36592 5; £10.00

Paths to Property
Approaches to Institutional Change in International Development
Karol Boudreaux & Paul Dragos Aligica
Hobart Paper 162; ISBN 978 0 255 36582 6; £10.00

Prohibitions
Edited by John Meadowcroft
Hobart Paperback 35; ISBN 978 0 255 36585 7; £15.00

Trade Policy, New Century
The WTO, FTAs and Asia Rising
Razeen Sally
Hobart Paper 163; ISBN 978 0 255 36544 4; £12.50

Sixty Years On – Who Cares for the NHS?
Helen Evans
Research Monograph 63; ISBN 978 0 255 36611 3; £10.00

Taming Leviathan
Waging the War of Ideas Around the World
Edited by Colleen Dyble
Occasional Paper 142; ISBN 978 0 255 36607 6; £12.50

The Legal Foundations of Free Markets
Edited by Stephen F. Copp
Hobart Paperback 36; ISBN 978 0 255 36591 8; £15.00

Climate Change Policy: Challenging the Activists
Edited by Colin Robinson
Readings 62; ISBN 978 0 255 36595 6; £10.00

Should We Mind the Gap?
Gender Pay Differentials and Public Policy
J. R. Shackleton
Hobart Paper 164; ISBN 978 0 255 36604 5; £10.00

Pension Provision: Government Failure Around the World
Edited by Philip Booth et al.
Readings 63; ISBN 978 0 255 36602 1; £15.00

New Europe's Old Regions
Piotr Zientara
Hobart Paper 165; ISBN 978 0 255 36617 5; £12.50

Central Banking in a Free Society
Tim Congdon
Hobart Paper 166; ISBN 978 0 255 36623 6; £12.50

Verdict on the Crash: Causes and Policy Implications
Edited by Philip Booth
Hobart Paperback 37; ISBN 978 0 255 36635 9; £12.50

The European Institutions as an Interest Group
The Dynamics of Ever-Closer Union
Roland Vaubel
Hobart Paper 167; ISBN 978 0 255 36634 2; £10.00

An Adult Approach to Education
Alison Wolf
Hobart Paper 168; ISBN 978 0 255 36586 4; £10.00

Other IEA publications

Comprehensive information on other publications and the wider work of the IEA can be found at www.iea.org.uk. To order any publication please see below.

Personal customers

Orders from personal customers should be directed to the IEA:
Bob Layson
IEA
2 Lord North Street
FREEPOST LON10168
London SW1P 3YZ
Tel: 020 7799 8909. Fax: 020 7799 2137
Email: blayson@iea.org.uk

Trade customers

All orders from the book trade should be directed to the IEA's distributor:
Gazelle Book Services Ltd (IEA Orders)
FREEPOST RLYS-EAHU-YSCZ
White Cross Mills
Hightown
Lancaster LA1 4XS
Tel: 01524 68765, Fax: 01524 53232
Email: sales@gazellebooks.co.uk

IEA subscriptions

The IEA also offers a subscription service to its publications. For a single annual payment (currently £42.00 in the UK), subscribers receive every monograph the IEA publishes. For more information please contact:
Adam Myers
Subscriptions
IEA
2 Lord North Street
FREEPOST LON10168
London SW1P 3YZ
Tel: 020 7799 8920, Fax: 020 7799 2137
Email: amyers@iea.org.uk